Anxious Attachment Recovery:

Mastering Emotional Balance & Relationship Security - Breakthrough Strategies for Transformation

Amalia Rowans

Contents

Anxious Attachment Recovery

Disclaimer Notice:

This book is intended for informational purposes only. The views and opinions expressed within this book are the personal views of the author and should not be taken as professional advice. The author and publisher are not responsible for any actions the reader takes based on the information provided in this book. The strategies mentioned in this book may only be suitable for some and may lead to the desired outcome for some individuals. Readers should consult a professional before significantly changing their personal or professional life.

Introduction

As you turn these pages, you will find yourself on a path of deep self-exploration and recovery. "Anxious Attachment Recovery" is more than just a book; it's a companion on your journey toward understanding the intricate dance of attachment and how it shapes our relationships. We dive into the nuanced ways anxious attachment manifests, from the silent whispers of doubt to the loud echoes of fear, and how these forces can disrupt our connections with those we cherish most.

This guide is crafted to illuminate the patterns that have held you back, offering a blend of scientific research, psychological insights, and personal anecdotes that resonate with the struggles and triumphs of overcoming anxious attachment. Each chapter is designed to enlighten and empower you with practical, actionable strategies that pave the way for building secure, resilient bonds.

Embrace this journey as an opportunity to redefine your relationship with yourself and others. Through introspection, healing exercises, and a commitment to change, you will discover the keys to unlocking a life filled with more joy, trust, and meaningful connections. "Anxious Attachment Recovery" invites you to step into a world where relationships are not sources of anxiety and fear but foundations of strength and freedom.

Welcome to the first day of the rest of your life—a life where you are not defined by your fears but by the courage to overcome them.

Part I

Understanding Anxious Attachment

Definition, characteristics & styles of anxious attachment

Anxious attachment is a pervasive issue that affects countless individuals, profoundly influencing their relationships and interactions with others. This chapter aims to shed light on the nature of anxious attachment, its origins, characteristics, and impacts, providing a comprehensive overview for those seeking to navigate their path to recovery.

Attachment styles are patterns of behavior that develop in early childhood and shape how individuals perceive and interact in relationships throughout their lives. There are four main attachment styles: secure, anxious-preoccupied, dismissive-avoidant, and fearful-avoidant.

Secure Attachment: Individuals with a certain attachment style feel comfortable with emotional intimacy and easily trust others. They are confident in themselves and their relationships, have practical communication skills, and can navigate conflicts constructively.

Anxious-Preoccupied Attachment: People with an anxious-preoccupied attachment style crave closeness and intimacy but often worry about their partner's availability and commitment. They may be overly sensitive to signs of rejection or abandonment, leading to clingy or demanding behavior.

Dismissive-Avoidant Attachment: Those with a dismissive-avoidant attachment style tend to prioritize independence and self-reliance. They may downplay the importance of close relationships, avoid emotional vulnerability, and struggle with intimacy and commitment.
Fearful-Avoidant Attachment: Individuals with a fearful-avoidant attachment style exhibit anxious and avoidant tendencies. They desire emotional connection but also

fear rejection and may push others away as a defense mechanism to protect themselves from getting hurt.

Understanding attachment styles can provide valuable insights into relationship dynamics, including communication patterns, conflict resolution strategies, and emotional needs.

Anxious attachment, also known as anxious-preoccupied attachment, is one of the four main attachment styles identified in attachment theory. It typically develops in early childhood in response to inconsistent or unpredictable caregiving, where the child's needs for comfort and security are not consistently met. As a result, individuals with an anxious attachment style tend to exhibit specific defining characteristics:

Fear of Abandonment: People with anxious attachment often

harbor deep-seated fears of being abandoned or rejected by their loved ones. They may worry excessively about the stability and permanence of their relationships, leading to clingy or dependent behavior.

Need for Reassurance: Individuals with anxious attachment frequently seek reassurance and validation from their partners to alleviate their fears and insecurities. They may require constant affirmation of their partner's love and commitment, often feeling anxious or distressed without such reassurance.

Hypersensitivity to Rejection: Anxiously attached individuals

are highly attuned to signs of rejection or disapproval from their partners. They may interpret minor conflicts or perceived slights as evidence of impending abandonment, leading to heightened emotional reactions and distress.

Intense Emotional Responses: People with anxious attachment

often experience extreme emotional highs and lows in their relationships. They may oscillate between moments of deep connection and overwhelming anxiety, driven by their fear of losing the relationship or being left alone.

Overdependence on Relationships: Anxious attachment is characterized by a strong desire for closeness and connection with others. Individuals with this attachment style may rely heavily on their relationships to fulfill their emotional needs, sometimes at the expense of their autonomy and self-esteem.

Overall, anxious attachment reflects a deep-seated insecurity and fear of rejection that can profoundly impact individuals' relationships and emotional well-being.

Understanding these behaviors is crucial for individuals to navigate their way toward healthier dynamics in relationships. By recognizing and addressing the underlying fears and patterns, those with anxious attachment can work towards developing a sense of security within themselves and their relationships. Therapy, self-reflection, and communication skills are often critical components in managing anxious attachment, enabling individuals to build stronger, more stable connections with their partners.

How anxious attachment forms in early life

Attachment is an emotional bond between infants and their primary caregivers. This bond is crucial for the child's development and affects their social, emotional, and cognitive development.

Anxious attachment often forms in early life as a result of inconsistent or unpredictable caregiving experiences during infancy and childhood. These experiences shape the child's beliefs about themselves, others, and relationships, laying the foundation for their attachment style. Anxious attachment, a pattern developed in early childhood, profoundly affects adult relationships and is characterized by a fear of abandonment and a constant need for reassurance. This attachment style originates from inconsistent caregiving, leading individuals to become hyper-vigilant about the security of their relationships.

When caregivers are inconsistently responsive or overly protective, children may feel anxious about the reliability of close bonds. This early conditioning leads to a heightened sensitivity to relational cues and a deep-seated fear of abandonment, which can persist into adulthood, affecting interpersonal relationships.

Children with anxious attachment may exhibit clingy behavior, seek constant validation, and struggle with self-regulation in the absence of their caregiver. As these individuals grow, their early attachment experiences can influence their self-esteem, relationship dynamics, and emotional coping strategies. Anxiously attached individuals often find themselves in a cycle of seeking closeness and reassurance while simultaneously fearing rejection and loss.

The psychology behind anxious attachment is rooted in early childhood experiences and the development of attachment patterns that shape individuals' relationship dynamics throughout their lives. Anxious attachment, also known as anxious-preoccupied attachment, is characterized by a strong desire for closeness and intimacy combined with fears of rejection and abandonment. Several key psychological factors contribute to the formation of anxious attachment:

Early Caregiving Experiences: Anxious attachment often develops in response to inconsistent or unpredictable caregiving during infancy and childhood. When caregivers are inconsistently responsive to a child's needs, the child learns to associate closeness and intimacy with anxiety and uncertainty.

This can lead to a persistent fear of abandonment and a heightened sensitivity to relational cues.

Internal Working Models: As children internalize their early caregiving experiences, they develop internal working models of relationships that shape their beliefs about themselves and others. Anxiously attached individuals may develop negative internal working models characterized by beliefs such as "I am unworthy of love" or "Others will inevitably leave me." These beliefs influence their expectations and behaviors in adult relationships.

Hyperactivation of Attachment System: Anxious attachment is associated with hyperactivation of the attachment system, meaning that individuals are hypersensitive to relational threats and constantly monitor their proximity to attachment figures. This hyperactivation can lead to heightened emotional reactivity, intense fear of rejection, and a strong desire for reassurance and closeness.

Regulation of Emotions: Anxious attachment is often accompanied by difficulties in emotion regulation, as individuals may struggle to manage intense feelings of anxiety, insecurity, and fear of abandonment. This can manifest in clinginess, neediness, and emotional volatility in relationships.

Fear of Rejection and Abandonment: At the core of anxious attachment is a profound fear of rejection and abandonment. This fear is rooted in early experiences of inconsistent caregiving and leads individuals to seek constant reassurance and validation from their partners to alleviate their anxiety. However, despite maintaining closeness, anxiously attached individuals may inadvertently push their partners away with clinginess and neediness.

Understanding the psychology behind anxious attachment can help individuals recognize and address maladaptive relationship patterns, cultivate self-awareness, and develop healthier ways of relating to others. Through therapy, self-reflection, and developing interpersonal skills, individuals can learn to challenge negative beliefs, regulate their emotions more effectively, and build more secure and fulfilling relationships.

Attachment theory

Attachment theory is a psychological, evolutionary, and ethological theory concerning relationships between humans. It was first developed during the 1950s by John Bowlby, a British psychoanalyst seeking to understand the intense distress experienced by infants who had been separated from their parents. Later, Mary Ainsworth, an American-Canadian developmental psychologist, expanded on Bowlby's work through her research, notably the "Strange Situation" assessment, which helped identify different attachment patterns between infants and their caregivers. Here are some of the fundamental concepts of attachment theory:

Secure Base: The theory posits that the primary caregiver acts as a secure base from which the child can explore the world. A secure base is essential for the development of independence and self-confidence.

Safe Haven: In times of fear or distress, the caregiver provides a haven to which the child can return for comfort and soothing.

Attachment Styles: Research by Ainsworth and others identified four primary attachment styles based on how infants respond to the presence, absence, and return of their caregiver:

Secure Attachment: Securely attached children usually show distress when their caregiver leaves but are happy upon their return, feeling assured that their needs will be met.

Avoidant Attachment: These children tend to avoid or ignore the caregiver, showing little emotion when the caregiver departs or returns. They learn to be self-sufficient.

Ambivalent (or Anxious) Attachment: These children become very distressed when a caregiver leaves and may not be consoled quickly upon return. They seek closeness to the caregiver but are not easily comforted.

Disorganized Attachment: A pattern characterized by a lack of apparent attachment behavior. These children may show a mixture of avoidance and resistance or seem dazed and confused. This style is often associated with inconsistent or traumatic caregiving.

Internal Working Models: Attachment theory suggests that early interactions with caregivers form the basis for internal working models of relationships. These models guide individuals' expectations, emotions, and behaviors in relationships throughout life.

The Importance of Sensitivity: The caregiver's sensitivity to the child's needs and signals is critical in developing a secure attachment. Responsive caregiving supports secure attachment when the caregiver accurately interprets the child's signals and responds appropriately and consistently.

Long-term Impact: The attachment style developed in early childhood can influence a wide range of outcomes, from self-esteem and emotional regulation to the quality of future relationships, including those with friends, romantic partners, and one's children.

Attachment theory has been instrumental in understanding the importance of early relationships in human development. It has applications in various fields, including psychology, education, child care, and psychotherapy, guiding interventions to support secure attachments and address issues stemming from insecure attachments.

Several factors contribute to the development of anxious attachment:

Caregiver Responsiveness: Anxiously attached individuals typically have caregivers who are inconsistently responsive to their needs. They may experience periods of nurturing and affection interspersed with times of emotional unavailability or neglect. This inconsistency creates confusion and anxiety for the child, as they cannot predict when their needs will be met.

Parental Availability: Anxious attachment can also develop when caregivers are emotionally unavailable or preoccupied with their concerns, leaving the child feeling neglected or unimportant. This lack of consistent emotional support undermines the child's sense of security and erodes their trust in their caregivers to provide comfort and reassurance.

Parental Rejection or Criticism: Children who experience rejection, criticism, or invalidation from their caregivers may develop anxious attachment as a defensive response to the perceived threat of abandonment. They may internalize negative messages about themselves, leading to low self-esteem and a heightened fear of rejection in future relationships.

Traumatic Experiences: Traumatic events such as loss, separation, or abuse during childhood can also contribute to the development of anxious attachment. These experiences can disrupt the child's sense of safety and security, leading to hypervigilance and anxiety in relationships.

Modeling of Attachment Behaviors: Children learn about relationships by observing and internalizing the behaviors of their primary caregivers. If caregivers exhibit anxious or insecure attachment patterns themselves, children may adopt similar behaviors as they navigate their relationships.

Overall, anxious attachment forms in early life as an adaptive response to the child's caregiving environment, characterized by inconsistency, emotional unavailability, or perceived threat. These early experiences shape the child's beliefs and expectations about relationships, influencing their attachment style and interpersonal dynamics throughout adulthood.

A deep fear of abandonment, excessive neediness, and a constant search for validation and reassurance from partners characterize anxious attachment. It stems from early childhood experiences with caregivers who were inconsistently available or responsive, leading individuals to become hyper-vigilant about their relationships' stability in adulthood. Those with anxious attachment often struggle with low self-esteem, are highly sensitive to partners' moods and actions, and may exhibit clinginess or possessiveness as a means to secure their connections.

Adults with anxious attachment may experience intense emotional reactions, difficulty trusting partners, and a tendency to remain in unsatisfying relationships due to their fear of being alone. Recognizing and understanding anxious attachment's nuances is the first step toward healing. Recovery involves identifying triggers, improving self-awareness, and developing healthier communication and emotional regulation strategies. By addressing these underlying issues, individuals can move towards forming secure, fulfilling relationships.

To navigate the path from anxious attachment formed in early life to secure relationships in adulthood, it's essential to understand its impact on emotional development and attachment behaviors. By addressing these early experiences, individuals can engage in therapeutic processes and practices that foster healthier attachment styles, laying the groundwork for more secure and fulfilling relationships. This journey often involves learning new ways to communicate needs and emotions effectively, as well as developing strategies to manage anxiety and insecurity in healthy ways.

Empowering oneself with knowledge and self-awareness allows for gradually replacing old patterns with new, secure ways of connecting. This transformative process enables individuals to move towards relationships where trust, mutual respect, and emotional availability are the cornerstones, ultimately leading to healthier, more satisfying connections that transcend the fears instilled in early life.

The impact of anxious attachment on adult relationships

The impact of anxious attachment on adult relationships is profoundly, affecting communication, intimacy, and trust. Adults with anxious attachment may experience heightened fears of abandonment, leading to behaviors that can push partners away, such as clinginess, excessive neediness, and constant requests for reassurance.

The fear of abandonment in adult relationships is a profound concern that affects many, leading to behaviors that can both strain and sabotage connections. This fear often manifests as a need for constant reassurance, sensitivity to changes in a partner's mood or behavior, and a tendency towards clinginess or possessiveness. Individuals may react preemptively to perceived threats of loss, which can create a self-fulfilling prophecy where their fears of abandonment lead to the very outcomes they wish to avoid. The impact on relationship dynamics can be significant, leading to cycles of conflict, emotional distance, and dissatisfaction.

To delve deeper into the fear of abandonment in adult relationships, it's essential to understand its origins, often rooted in early life experiences. Individuals carrying this fear into their adult relationships may exhibit behaviors such as excessive jealousy, seeking constant validation, and difficulty being alone. These behaviors can strain relationships, as partners may feel overwhelmed or unable to meet the continuous demands for reassurance.

This attachment style challenges relationship stability, but understanding and addressing these patterns through therapy, communication, and self-awareness can foster healthier, more secure connections. Recognizing and mitigating the effects of anxious attachment is crucial for cultivating lasting, fulfilling relationships.

People with anxious attachment often exhibit heightened sensitivity to their partner's moods and actions due to their deep fear of abandonment and rejection. This sensitivity stems from their constant vigilance for signs that their relationship may be in jeopardy. They may interpret even minor changes in their partner's behavior as evidence of cooling affection or a precursor to abandonment, which can lead to miscommunications and conflicts within the relationship. This vigilance is a protective strategy aimed at preempting potential hurt, but it can also create a self-fulfilling prophecy that strains the relationship.

Their heightened sensitivity is not merely emotional but also a cognitive bias, making them more likely to notice and interpret neutral actions negatively. This heightened state of alertness to relational cues is driven by an underlying anxiety about the stability of their connections. Consequently, they may respond to these perceived threats with behaviors aimed at securing reassurance and closeness, which can inadvertently create tension and conflict, further destabilizing the relationship they wish to preserve. This cycle is rooted in early experiences where the consistency of emotional support was uncertain, leading them to be perpetually on guard in adult relationships.

Anxiously attached individuals' sensitivity to their partner's moods and actions also impacts their self-regulation and emotional processing. Their constant monitoring for signs of disapproval or disinterest can lead to heightened emotional reactions. It may prompt behaviors more about soothing their anxieties than responding to their partner's feelings or needs. This pattern can erode trust and mutual respect, making building a stable, fulfilling relationship challenging. Recognizing and addressing this sensitivity through therapy or mindfulness practices can help develop healthier ways of relating and responding to partners.

People with attachment anxiety might sabotage their relationships through constant need for reassurance, leading to their partner feeling overwhelmed. They may interpret neutral actions negatively, causing unnecessary conflicts. Overreacting to minor issues, fearing abandonment at any sign of independence from their partner, and seeking to merge identities can push partners away. These behaviors, rooted in fear rather than relationship issues, can create a cycle of self-fulfilling prophecies where anxiously attached individuals inadvertently bring about the rejection they fear.

Communication patterns in relationships are crucial for maintaining a healthy connection. Effective communication fosters understanding, empathy, and support, while poor communication can lead to misunderstandings, resentment, and conflict. Patterns such as active listening, open and honest expression of feelings and needs, and non-defensive responses promote stronger bonds. Conversely, negative patterns like avoidance, criticism, contempt, and stonewalling can erode trust and intimacy. Recognizing and adjusting these patterns are essential to building a more fulfilling and resilient relationship.

Developing positive communication patterns involves cultivating habits that promote clarity, compassion, and connection. Techniques such as reflective listening, where one partner mirrors back what the other has said, can enhance understanding and validation. Expressing needs and desires directly and respectfully, without accusation or blame, encourages constructive dialogue. Recognizing and pausing during escalating conflicts allows for calmer, more effective communication. A communication environment where both partners feel heard, valued, and respected is vital to deepening the relational bond and navigating challenges together.

Effective communication also involves recognizing and adapting to each other's communication styles. Understanding that individuals express and interpret messages differently can prevent many misunderstandings. Establishing a culture of gratitude and appreciation in daily interactions strengthens emotional connections, making it easier to navigate difficult conversations. Regularly dedicating time to discuss relationship needs and concerns outside conflict situations helps maintain alignment and mutual understanding. Integrating these practices fosters a resilient and supportive relationship environment conducive to growth and deep connection.

To further enhance communication in relationships, it's crucial to practice emotional intelligence, which includes recognizing one's emotions and those of the partner, managing emotions constructively, and empathizing with the partner's perspective. Developing conflict resolution skills that focus on finding mutual solutions rather than winning arguments can transform conflicts into opportunities for growth. Additionally, celebrating each other's successes and supporting each other through challenges strengthens the bond. Prioritizing open, honest, and empathetic communication creates a foundation of trust and intimacy, which is essential for a thriving relationship.

People with attachment anxiety often face communication challenges, including difficulty in expressing their needs due to fear of rejection or conflict. This fear can lead to avoiding discussions about their concerns, which might escalate misunderstandings. Additionally, their intense fear of conflict may prevent them from addressing issues directly, opting for indirect communication that can be misinterpreted. Such patterns hinder the resolution of problems and prevent the deepening of intimacy and trust in relationships.

Identifying triggers that evoke anxiety

Identifying triggers that evoke anxiety involves recognizing specific situations, thoughts, or behaviors that consistently lead to feelings of fear, worry, or stress. These triggers can vary widely from person to person and may be related to past experiences, current stressors, or internalized beliefs. Some common triggers of anxiety include:

Social Situations: Interactions with unfamiliar people, large crowds, or social events can trigger anxiety, especially for individuals with social anxiety disorder.

Performance Pressure: The pressure to perform well academically, professionally, or socially can trigger anxiety, leading to feelings of inadequacy or fear of failure.

Uncertainty: Ambiguous or unpredictable situations, such as changes in routine, decision-making, or future planning, can evoke anxiety due to the lack of control or predictability.

Conflict or Criticism: Confrontation, criticism, or disapproval from others can trigger anxiety, particularly for individuals with a fear of rejection or abandonment.

Health Concerns: Worries about illness, injury, or medical procedures can evoke anxiety, especially for individuals with health-related anxiety disorders.

Trauma Triggers: Certain sights, sounds, smells, or memories associated with past traumatic experiences can trigger anxiety and distressing emotions.

Time Pressure: Deadlines, time constraints, or feeling rushed can trigger anxiety, leading to feelings of overwhelm or panic.

Perfectionism: The desire to be flawless or meet unrealistic standards can trigger anxiety, as individuals may fear making mistakes or falling short of expectations.

Identifying these triggers involves paying attention to patterns of thoughts, emotions, and physical sensations that arise in response to specific situations or stimuli. Keeping a journal, seeking feedback from trusted individuals, or working with a therapist can help uncover and understand your unique triggers for anxiety.

Once identified, learning coping strategies and practicing relaxation techniques can help manage anxiety when faced with these triggers.

Scenario: Sarah's Anxiety Triggers

Trigger: Public Speaking

Sarah experiences intense anxiety whenever she has to speak in front of a group of people, whether it's in a classroom setting, a business presentation, or even during a casual gathering.

Symptoms: Sarah's heart races, she starts sweating profusely, her hands tremble, and she finds it difficult to articulate her thoughts coherently. She often experiences a sense of impending doom and feels like she might faint or embarrass herself in front of others.

Thoughts: Sarah constantly worries about being judged negatively by others. She fears that she will make a mistake, stumble over her words, or forget what she wants to say. She worries about being perceived as incompetent or unintelligent.

Physical Sensations: Sarah experiences a tightness in her chest, shortness of breath, and a knot in her stomach whenever she anticipates having to speak in public. She feels a surge of adrenaline coursing through her body, which only amplifies her feelings of panic.

Behavioral Responses: Sarah often avoids situations that require public speaking whenever possible. She may make excuses to skip presentations or delegate speaking tasks to others. When she cannot avoid speaking in public, she may resort to excessive preparation or use coping mechanisms such as deep breathing exercises or visualization techniques to manage her anxiety.

Impact on Daily Life: Sarah's fear of public speaking significantly impacts her personal and professional life. It hinders her ability to advance in her career, as she avoids opportunities that involve presenting ideas or leading meetings. It also affects her social life, as she may decline invitations to social events where she knows she'll be expected to speak in front of others.

Coping Strategies: Sarah seeks therapy to address her anxiety around public speaking. Through cognitive-behavioral therapy (CBT), she learns to challenge and reframe negative thoughts about her abilities. She also practices exposure therapy, gradually exposing herself to speaking in front of others in a supportive environment to desensitize herself to the fear.

In this example, Sarah's trigger for anxiety is public speaking. By breaking down the various aspects of her experience surrounding this trigger, including symptoms, thoughts, physical sensations, behavioral responses, and its impact on her daily life, we gain a comprehensive understanding of how anxiety manifests for her in this particular situation. Additionally, we explore potential coping strategies she might employ to manage her anxiety effectively.

Part II

Recognizing Anxious Attachment

Signs of Anxious Attachment in Relationships

Signs of anxious attachment in relationships include:

Needing constant reassurance from partners.

Fear of abandonment leads to clinginess.

Difficulty trusting partners.

Overanalyzing minor issues as signs of relationship problems.

These behaviors stem from deep-seated fears and insecurities, often leading to a cycle of dependency and tension within the relationship.

To understand if your partner is anxiously attached, observe if they frequently seek reassurance about your feelings, show intense fear of losing you, react strongly to perceived changes in your affection, have difficulty trusting you entirely, or cling to the relationship despite issues. These behaviors reflect underlying anxieties about abandonment and self-worth.

To further understand if your partner has an anxious attachment, consider how they handle separations or time apart. Anxiously attached individuals may experience significant distress when apart from their partner, leading to frequent texts or calls. They might also need help with independence within the relationship, preferring to do most activities together.

Recognizing these signs can help in addressing the needs of an anxiously attached partner, promoting healthier communication and boundaries in the relationship.

Anxiously attached partners might also show a high sensitivity to criticism, perceiving it as a threat to the relationship. This sensitivity can lead to defensiveness or an exaggerated emotional response to what might be considered minor feedback. Additionally, they may prioritize the relationship above their needs or interests, fearing that asserting themselves could harm their partner.

Understanding these behaviors can foster empathy and guide supportive responses that help strengthen the relationship.

When trying to understand the nuances of anxious attachment in relationships, it's crucial to observe how your partner reacts to conflict and stress. An anxiously attached individual might often anticipate rejection or disappointment, which can lead them to preemptively address or sometimes even create issues that might not exist. They may also have difficulty enjoying positive moments in the relationship because they worry about the future.

Clinginess and neediness

Clinginess and possessiveness in relationships often stem from deep-rooted fears of abandonment and insecurity. Clingy behavior manifests as a constant need for attention and reassurance, while possessiveness reflects an intense fear of losing the partner to someone else. These traits can suffocate the space needed for a healthy, independent relationship, leading to tension and potentially driving partners away.

Possessiveness can escalate into controlling behavior, eroding the foundation of trust and respect that healthy relationships require. Such behaviors cause discomfort and strain and lead to a cycle of dependency and resentment. It's vital for individuals displaying these traits to seek understanding and healing through therapy to address underlying insecurities and fears. Developing self-confidence and fostering trust can help alleviate the need for constant reassurance and control, leading to more balanced and fulfilling relationships.

When clinginess and possessiveness are not addressed, they can significantly hinder personal growth and the development of a secure self-identity. Individuals may seek validation through their relationships rather than cultivating their interests and self-worth independently. This dynamic can lead to a lack of fulfillment and personal autonomy, making it crucial for those experiencing these feelings to engage in self-exploration and to build a sense of security from within.

Neediness in relationships also stems from a deep fear of abandonment and a lack of self-esteem, leading individuals to seek constant validation and assurance from their partners. This behavior can strain relationships, placing undue pressure on partners to fulfill emotional voids. Addressing neediness involves building self-confidence, fostering independence, and developing healthy communication habits to express needs without imposing them on others.

To further address neediness, it's essential to understand that it affects not only romantic relationships but also friendships and family dynamics. Individuals exhibiting needy behavior may fear being alone and often rely heavily on others for emotional support, approval, and identity. Working on self-awareness, engaging in activities that promote self-reliance, and establishing boundaries are crucial steps toward overcoming neediness.

Neediness can manifest in various ways, such as constantly seeking reassurance, feeling anxious when apart from your partner, or struggling with feelings of jealousy or insecurity. These behaviors can create a sense of suffocation in the relationship, as people in need may rely heavily on their partner for their emotional well-being. Moreover, neediness can lead to a cycle of seeking validation from others to feel worthy rather than cultivating self-confidence from within. Recognizing the underlying fears and insecurities driving neediness is crucial for fostering personal growth and developing healthier relationships. This often involves exploring past experiences and building a stronger self-worth and autonomy. By addressing these issues, individuals can cultivate more fulfilling and balanced relationships based on mutual respect and support.

Overcoming the Fear of Being Abandoned and Rejected

Overcoming the fear of abandonment and rejection is a gradual process that involves self-awareness, self-compassion, and intentional practice. Here are some steps that can help:

Recognize and Validate Your Feelings: Acknowledge that your fear of abandonment and rejection is valid and understandable, given your past experiences. Allow yourself to feel and express your emotions without judgment.

Challenge Negative Thoughts: Notice when you're engaging in self-critical or catastrophizing thinking patterns related to abandonment and rejection. Challenge these thoughts by questioning their validity and replacing them with more balanced and realistic perspectives.

Build Self-Esteem: Work on cultivating a positive self-image and recognizing your worth independent of others' opinions or actions. Practice self-care set personal boundaries, and engage in activities that bring you joy and fulfillment.

Develop Secure Relationships: Surround yourself with supportive and trustworthy individuals who demonstrate consistent care and respect for your feelings. Building secure attachments with others can help counteract feelings of insecurity and fear.

Practice Mindfulness: Mindfulness techniques, such as meditation and deep breathing exercises, can help you stay grounded in the present moment and reduce anxiety about the future. Mindfulness can also enhance self-awareness and self-compassion.

Seek Therapy: Consider working with a therapist specializing in attachment issues or cognitive-behavioral therapy (CBT). Therapy can provide a safe space to explore your fears, identify underlying patterns, and develop coping strategies to manage them effectively.

Challenge Your Comfort Zone: Gradually expose yourself to situations that trigger feelings of abandonment or rejection, starting with small, manageable steps. Over time, you'll build resilience and confidence in coping with uncertainty and discomfort.

Remember that overcoming the fear of abandonment and rejection is a journey, and it's okay to progress at your own pace. Be patient and gentle with yourself as you navigate this process, and celebrate your progress.

Overanalyzing relationship dynamics

Overanalyzing relationship dynamics involves excessively scrutinizing and interpreting every aspect of the relationship, often leading to unnecessary stress and anxiety. This behavior can stem from various factors, including insecurity, fear of rejection, or a need for control. Some common signs of overanalyzing relationship dynamics include:

Constantly Ruminating: An individual may obsess over past conversations, actions, or interactions with their partner, analyzing them for hidden meanings or potential signs of trouble.

Reading Into Small Details: Overanalyzing individuals may assign exaggerated significance to minor events or gestures, interpreting them as indicators of the health or stability of the relationship.

Seeking Reassurance: Anxious individuals may repeatedly seek reassurance from their partner or others about the state of the relationship, often due to persistent doubts or fears.

Fear of Uncertainty: Overanalyzing individuals may struggle with uncertainty and ambiguity in the relationship, feeling the need to constantly "figure things out" to alleviate their anxiety.

Difficulty Trusting: Individuals who overanalyze may need help to trust their partner fully, questioning their motives or intentions even without evidence of wrongdoing.

Perfectionism: Overanalyzing individuals may have unrealistic expectations for the relationship, striving for an unattainable level of perfection and becoming overly critical when things don't meet their standards.

Overanalyzing relationship dynamics can strain the relationship and create unnecessary tension between partners. It's essential for individuals to recognize when they are engaging in this behavior and to take steps to address it. This may involve practicing mindfulness to stay present in the moment, challenging negative thought patterns, and communicating openly and honestly with their partner about their concerns. Seeking support from a therapist or counselor can

also be beneficial in learning healthier ways to navigate relationship dynamics and manage anxiety.

Overcoming overanalyzing in relationships involves developing self-awareness, practicing mindfulness, and adopting healthier coping strategies.

Recognize Your Patterns: Become aware of when you start overanalyzing your relationship dynamics. Notice the thoughts, emotions, and behaviors that accompany this pattern.

Challenge Negative Thoughts: When you catch yourself overanalyzing, challenge the validity of your thoughts. Ask yourself if there is evidence to support your assumptions or if you might be misinterpreting the situation.

Practice Mindfulness: Stay present and focus on what is happening now, rather than getting lost in hypothetical scenarios or future worries. Mindfulness techniques, such as deep breathing or meditation, can help you stay grounded.

Communicate Openly: Instead of expressing your concerns, communicate openly and honestly with your partner about your thoughts and feelings. Share your insecurities and fears in a constructive and non-blaming manner.

Set Boundaries: Establish healthy boundaries for yourself and your relationship. Recognize when you need space or time to process your thoughts and emotions and communicate these needs to your partner.

Engage in Self-Care: Take care of your physical, emotional, and mental well-being. Engage in activities that bring you joy and relaxation, and prioritize self-care practices that help you manage stress and anxiety.

Seek Support: Consider seeking support from a therapist or counselor who can help you explore the underlying causes of your overanalyzing behavior and develop effective coping strategies.

Focus on the Positive: Cultivate gratitude and appreciation for the positive aspects of your relationship. Remind yourself of your partner's strengths and why you value your connection.

By practicing these strategies consistently, you can gradually reduce overanalyzing and cultivate a healthier and more fulfilling relationship dynamic. Remember that change takes time and patience, so be gentle with yourself as you work towards overcoming this pattern.

The role of past trauma and experiences

The role of past trauma and experiences in an individual's life is profound, influencing mental health, behavior, relationships, and overall well-being. Trauma can arise from a variety of experiences, including but not limited to abuse, neglect, loss, accidents, natural disasters, war, and witnessing violence. The impact of these experiences can be far-reaching, affecting individuals differently based on their resilience, support systems, and biological predispositions. Understanding the role of past trauma and experiences is crucial in fields such as psychology, psychiatry, social work, and education. Here are some critical aspects of how past trauma and experiences play a role in an individual's life:

Psychological Impact: Trauma can lead to a range of psychological issues, including post-traumatic stress disorder (PTSD), anxiety disorders, depression, substance abuse, and personality disorders. The severity and duration of these conditions can vary widely and may emerge immediately after the traumatic event or years later.

Influence on Behavior: Individuals who have experienced trauma may exhibit changes in behavior, such as increased aggression, withdrawal from social interactions, or risky behaviors. These behavioral changes are often coping mechanisms or ways of dealing with unresolved trauma.

Impact on Relationships: Trauma can affect an individual's ability to form and maintain healthy relationships. Trust issues, fear of intimacy, and difficulty in communicating emotions are common challenges faced by those with a history of trauma. This can lead to patterns of attachment that are insecure, such as avoidant or anxious attachment, impacting both personal and professional relationships.

Physical Health Consequences: There is a growing body of research indicating that trauma, especially chronic stress or childhood trauma, can have significant physical health consequences. This includes increased risk for chronic conditions such as heart disease, diabetes, and autoimmune diseases, as well as impacting immune function and sleep patterns.

Cognitive Effects: Trauma can affect cognitive functions, including attention, memory, and executive functioning. It may lead to difficulties in learning, memory recall, and decision-making processes. In children, this can affect academic performance and social development.

Resilience and Recovery: Individuals respond to trauma in diverse ways. Factors such as a supportive social network, access to therapy or counseling, and personal resilience can influence the recovery process. Some people find that working through trauma can lead to personal growth and increased resilience, a phenomenon known as post-traumatic growth.

Therapeutic Approaches: Addressing the impact of past trauma is a critical component of therapeutic interventions. Approaches such as trauma-focused cognitive behavioral therapy (TF-CBT), eye movement desensitization and reprocessing (EMDR), and mindfulness-based therapies are effective in treating trauma-related symptoms.

Importance of Early Intervention: Early identification and intervention can mitigate the long-term effects of trauma. This includes providing support and resources to those at risk, such as children exposed to adverse childhood experiences (ACEs), to prevent the development of more severe mental health issues.

Understanding the role of past trauma and experiences is essential for developing effective strategies for prevention, intervention, and support for those affected. It underscores the importance of a holistic approach to well-being, recognizing the interconnection between mental, emotional, physical, and social health.

The brain and anxious attachment

The relationship between the brain and anxious attachment—characterized by intense fears of abandonment and preoccupation with the availability of close relational partners—reflects a complex interplay of neurobiological, psychological, and environmental factors. Anxious attachment, one of the patterns identified within attachment theory, can significantly impact an individual's emotional regulation and relationship behavior. Research into the neural underpinnings of anxious attachment has highlighted several key areas and processes in the brain that contribute to this attachment style:

Amygdala: The amygdala is crucial in processing emotional reactions and mainly involves fear and anxiety responses. Individuals with an anxious attachment style may have an amygdala that is more easily activated or less regulated, leading to heightened emotional responses to perceived threats of separation or rejection.

Pre-frontal Cortex (PFC): The PFC is involved in executive functions, such as decision-making, impulse control, and emotional regulation. Differences in the functioning or structure of the PFC in anxiously attached individuals may contribute to difficulties in regulating emotions and responses to stress, leading to more reactive behaviors in relationships.

Anterior Cingulate Cortex (ACC): The ACC is involved in processing emotional pain and social rejection. Studies suggest that individuals with an anxious attachment may exhibit increased activity in the ACC in response to threats of loss or rejection, mirroring the pain of physical injury and contributing to the intense emotional distress experienced.

Hypothalamic-Pituitary-Adrenal (HPA) Axis: The HPA axis regulates the stress response through the release of cortisol. Research indicates that anxiously attached individuals may have a more reactive HPA axis, leading to heightened stress responses. This can affect their emotional regulation and stress management in relationship contexts.

Oxytocin and Vasopressin: These neuropeptides play roles in social bonding and attachment. Variations in the receptors for oxytocin and vasopressin have been linked to attachment styles. This suggests that differences in the oxytocin system may influence the development or expression of anxious attachment through effects on trust, bonding, and emotional regulation.

Neuroplasticity: Experiences in relationships, particularly early ones with primary caregivers, can shape the neural circuits associated with attachment and emotional regulation. Anxious attachments may develop partly due to earlier experiences that fail to adequately reassure or consistently meet emotional needs, leading to long-term changes in brain function and structure that influence attachment behaviors.

Understanding the neural basis of anxious attachment helps in developing targeted interventions. For example, therapies focusing on enhancing emotional regulation, such as mindfulness-based interventions or cognitive-behavioral approaches, may help rewire some neural pathways associated with anxious attachment. Moreover, understanding the role of the brain in attachment styles underscores the importance of supportive and responsive caregiving in early development and the potential for change and healing in the brain through positive relational experiences and therapeutic interventions.

Continuing from the discussion on the neural correlates of anxious attachment and its implications, it becomes evident that therapeutic and intervention strategies can be particularly effective when they address both the psychological and neurobiological dimensions of attachment issues. Given the brain's plasticity, interventions can lead to positive changes in emotional and behavioral patterns and the underlying neural mechanisms associated with anxious attachment. Here are some further considerations and interventions that can support individuals with an edgy attachment style:

Psychotherapy and Counseling

Cognitive Behavioral Therapy (CBT): CBT can help individuals recognize and challenge the negative thought patterns that often accompany anxious attachment, such as fears of abandonment or beliefs about unworthiness. CBT can support changes in emotional regulation and relationship behaviors by addressing these cognitive aspects.

Dialectical Behavior Therapy (DBT): DBT emphasizes skills in mindfulness, emotion regulation, distress tolerance, and interpersonal effectiveness. These skills are particularly beneficial for individuals with anxious attachment, helping them manage intense emotions and develop healthier relationship dynamics.

Attachment-based therapies: These therapies focus directly on understanding and addressing attachment patterns. Individuals can develop a more secure attachment style by exploring past relationship experiences and their impact on current behaviors. Therapists may use techniques to foster a corrective emotional experience, replicating the fast base function of attachment figures.

Mindfulness and Meditation

Mindfulness practices can help individuals with anxious attachments become more aware of their emotional responses and triggers without over-identifying with them. This increased awareness can promote emotional regulation and reduce reactivity in relationships. Mindfulness can also enhance one's capacity for self-compassion, which is crucial for healing attachment wounds.

Pharmacotherapy

In some cases, medication may be used as part of a comprehensive treatment plan, especially when anxiety symptoms are severe. SSRIs (selective serotonin reuptake inhibitors) or other anti-anxiety medications can help manage the symptoms of anxiety, making it easier for individuals to engage in psychotherapy and apply new coping strategies.

Social Support and Relationship Work

Building a supportive social network and engaging in healthy relationships can provide practical experience with secure attachment behaviors. Support groups, peer relationships, and therapeutic relationships can all serve as opportunities to experience trust, reliability, and emotional safety, which are vital for individuals working to overcome anxious attachment patterns.

Education and Self-awareness

Educating individuals about attachment styles and their impacts can empower them with the knowledge to understand their behaviors and feelings within the context of their relationships. Increased self-awareness is a critical first step in the change process, allowing individuals to recognize their needs and seek relationships supporting their growth toward security.

Addressing anxious attachment involves a multifaceted approach considering the individual's psychological needs, neurobiological underpinnings, and environmental factors. The goal of intervention is not just to alleviate symptoms but to foster a shift towards more secure attachment patterns, enhancing the individual's capacity for emotional regulation, resilience, and fulfilling relationships. With appropriate support and intervention, individuals with an anxious attachment style can develop healthier ways of relating to others and themselves, reflecting the remarkable capacity of the brain and psyche for growth and change.

Part III

The Impact of Anxious Attachment

Effects on Personal Well-being

In pursuing personal well-being, our lifestyle choices are pivotal in influencing our physical health, mental state, and overall quality of life. Well-being encompasses more than just the absence of disease; it is a complex blend of a person's physical, mental, emotional, and social health factors. It's about living a life full of personal fulfillment, joy, and purpose. This article explores the multifaceted effects of lifestyle choices on emotional well-being, underscoring the importance of holistic living and mindful decision-making.

Physical Health and Lifestyle Choices

Our physical health often lays the foundation of personal well-being. Choices related to diet, exercise, sleep, and substance use significantly impact our body's functioning and susceptibility to diseases. A balanced diet rich in nutrients supports bodily functions and combats illness, while regular physical activity strengthens the heart, muscles, and bones, enhancing overall vitality and energy levels. Adequate sleep is crucial for recovery, cognitive function, and emotional regulation. Conversely, habits such as smoking, excessive alcohol consumption, and drug use can lead to chronic diseases and diminish quality of life.

Mental and Emotional Well-being

Our lifestyle choices also have profound implications for our mental and emotional health. Activities that foster a sense of achievement, like mastering a new skill or involving social interaction, can significantly enhance mood and self-esteem. Mindfulness practices, such as meditation and yoga, have been shown to reduce stress, anxiety, and symptoms of depression, promoting a sense of inner peace.

Conversely, chronic stress—whether from overwork, financial pressures, or relationship issues—can lead to serious mental health problems, including depression and anxiety. The digital era has introduced the challenge of screen time management, with excessive use linked to increased loneliness, reduced sleep quality, and heightened anxiety levels.

Social Connections and Community Engagement

Humans are inherently social beings, and our relationships and community interactions significantly influence our well-being. Strong social connections are associated with reduced risk of mental health issues, lower stress levels, and longer lifespan. Engaging in community service or group activities provides a sense of belonging and purpose, contributing to higher happiness and satisfaction.

In contrast, isolation and poor relationship quality can lead to feelings of loneliness and decreased mental health, underscoring the importance of nurturing positive relationships and seeking supportive social networks.

Environmental Influences

The environment in which we live and work can significantly affect our well-being. Access to green spaces, such as parks and nature reserves, encourages physical activity and has been linked to lower stress levels, improved mood, and better mental health. Urban design and workplace environments that promote social interaction and physical activity can enhance community well-being and individual health.

Personal Development and Lifelong Learning

Engaging in continuous learning and personal development activities can provide a sense of achievement and confidence, positively impacting our well-being. Setting and working towards goals related to career advancement, personal interests, or skills development contributes to a sense of purpose and fulfillment.

Personal well-being is influenced by a complex interplay of factors, many of which are within our control. We can enhance our overall quality of life by making conscious lifestyle choices that promote physical health, mental and emotional well-being, social connectivity, environmental sustainability, and personal growth. It's about finding balance and harmony in our lives, continually striving for well-being that fosters happiness, health, and fulfillment.

Emotional regulation challenges

In the journey towards recovery from anxious attachment, one of the most significant hurdles individuals face is mastering emotional regulation. Anxious attachment, characterized by a pervasive fear of abandonment and an excessive need for reassurance, can lead to intense and overwhelming emotions. These emotional experiences often stem from early relationship dynamics that failed to provide a secure base, leading to difficulties managing emotions in adult relationships. This chapter delves into the challenges of emotional regulation in recovering from anxious attachment, offering insights into the mechanisms at play and strategies for overcoming these obstacles.

Understanding Emotional Regulation

Emotional regulation refers to the processes by which individuals influence which emotions they have, when they have them, and how they experience and express these emotions. It is a crucial aspect of mental health and well-being, impacting one's ability to cope with stress, maintain relationships, and navigate the complexities of daily life. For those with an anxious attachment style, emotional regulation can be particularly challenging, often resulting in heightened sensitivity to relationship cues and a propensity towards emotional intensity and reactivity.

The Role of the Brain

Research into the neural underpinnings of anxious attachment has highlighted specific brain regions implicated in emotional regulation challenges. The amygdala, known for its role in fear and emotional processing, is often more reactive in individuals with anxious attachment. This heightened reactivity can lead to an amplified response to perceived threats of abandonment or rejection. Additionally, variations in prefrontal cortex activity, which regulates emotional reactions, can further complicate the ability to modulate emotions effectively.

Triggers and Responses

For those with anxious attachment, common triggers include perceived distance or disengagement from a partner, criticism, or conflict. These situations can ignite a cascade of emotional responses, including anxiety, fear, and sadness, often disproportionate to the trigger. The challenge lies in the intensity of the emotions and the struggle to return to a state of emotional equilibrium.

Effects on Relationships

In the realm of anxious attachment recovery, understanding the profound impact this attachment style has on relationships is paramount. Anxious attachment, characterized by a deep fear of abandonment and an overwhelming need for reassurance, can significantly shape the dynamics of romantic partnerships, friendships, and familial bonds. This chapter delves into how anxious attachment influences these relationships, unraveling the patterns that can hinder connection and intimacy. It also offers strategies to foster healthier, more fulfilling interactions, paving the way for recovery and growth.

The Dynamics of Anxious Attachment in Relationships

Hyper-vigilance and Reassurance-seeking

Individuals with anxious attachment often exhibit hyper-vigilance to cues of rejection or abandonment in their relationships. This heightened sensitivity can lead to constant reassurance-seeking behaviors, where the individual requires frequent affirmations of love and commitment from their partners or friends. While such behaviors stem from a place of vulnerability, they can inadvertently strain relationships, leading to dependency and frustration.

Conflict and Communication

The fear of losing a significant other can drive individuals with anxious attachment towards behaviors that ironically push others away. Conflicts may arise from misunderstandings, where one partner's need for closeness overwhelms the other. Communication breakdowns are common, as anxiously attached individuals might struggle to express their needs healthily, fearing that assertiveness might lead to rejection.

Relationship Instability and Jealousy

Relationship instability and jealousy can be detrimental to the health and longevity of a partnership, leading to conflicts, mistrust, and emotional distress. Here's how these issues can manifest and some strategies for addressing them:

Relationship Instability:

Relationship instability is a lack of consistency, predictability, or security within a partnership. It may stem from various factors, including communication problems, unresolved conflicts, differences in values or goals, or external stressors. Signs of relationship instability may include frequent arguments, emotional distance, inconsistency in behaviors, and a lack of commitment or investment in the partnership.

The oscillation between clinging and pushing away can create a sense of instability within relationships. Anxious attachment can also manifest in jealousy and possessiveness, stemming from insecurities about the relationship's security and the partner's fidelity. Such dynamics can erode trust and mutual respect, undermining the foundation of the relationship.

Jealousy is a complex emotion that arises from fear of losing someone or feeling threatened by a perceived rival. It may stem from insecurity, past experiences of betrayal or abandonment, or unrealistic expectations within the relationship. Jealousy can manifest in various ways, including possessiveness, mistrust, insecurity, and controlling behaviors.

Navigating Recovery: Strategies for Healthier Relationships

Building Self-awareness

Recovery begins with self-awareness. Recognizing the patterns of anxious attachment and understanding their origins can empower individuals to start making changes. Reflecting on past relationships and identifying triggers for anxiety can provide valuable insights into how to approach current and future relationships differently.

Enhancing Communication Skills

Effective communication is a cornerstone of healthy relationships. Learning to express needs, fears, and desires openly and assertively, without expectation or demand, can significantly improve relational dynamics. Developing active listening skills is also crucial, ensuring that both partners feel heard and valued.

Cultivating Self-reliance

Strengthening self-reliance involves nurturing a sense of independence and confidence in one's ability to cope with life's challenges, including the prospect of being alone. Engaging in personal interests, building a supportive social network, and practicing self-care can reduce the dependency on a partner for emotional fulfillment and self-esteem.

Seeking Therapy

Therapy, especially with a focus on attachment issues, can be incredibly beneficial for individuals with anxious attachment. Therapies like Cognitive Behavioral Therapy (CBT), Dialectical Behavior Therapy (DBT), and Emotionally Focused Therapy (EFT) can help individuals understand their attachment style, develop healthier coping mechanisms, and build more secure relationships.

Fostering Secure Attachments

Creating secure attachments involves being mindful of the dynamics that promote security and intimacy in relationships. This includes consistent, responsive, and empathetic interactions with partners, friends, and family. It's about creating a balance between closeness and independence, where both individuals feel supported yet free to pursue their paths.

The journey towards recovering from anxious attachment and its effects on relationships is a path of profound personal growth and transformation. By understanding the impact of anxious attachment on relational dynamics, individuals can begin to untangle the patterns that have held them back, embracing new ways of connecting rooted in security, communication, and mutual respect. Through self-awareness, therapeutic support, and a commitment to change, it is possible to cultivate relationships that are nourishing, stable, and deeply fulfilling, marking a new chapter in the story of recovery.

Patterns of co-dependency

Co-dependency, a term often intertwined with discussions of anxious attachment, refers to a relationship dynamic where one person's sense of purpose and self-worth becomes excessively entangled with the needs, approval, and presence of another person. This dynamic is particularly prevalent among individuals with anxious attachment styles, who may find themselves in cycles of co-dependency in their quest for security and reassurance. This chapter explores the nature of co-dependent patterns in the context of anxious attachment, highlighting the challenges they present and offering pathways towards healthier, more autonomous relationships.

The Nexus Between Anxious Attachment and Co-dependency

Anxious attachment, with its core features of fear of abandonment and craving for closeness, sets the stage for co-dependent relationships. Individuals with this attachment style may unconsciously seek out partners who, in some way, affirm their fears and dependencies, thereby reinforcing the cycle of co-dependency. These relationships often feature an imbalance, where the anxiously attached individual invests a disproportionate amount of their emotional energy in managing the relationship and the other person's well-being at their own expense.

Identifying Co-dependent Behaviors

Co-dependent behaviors can manifest in various ways, including but not limited to:

- Overwhelming Need for Approval: Basing one's self-esteem and decisions on the approval of a partner or loved one.
- Sacrificing One's Needs: Consistently putting the partner's needs above one's own, often neglecting personal well-being, interests, and boundaries.
- Fear of Abandonment: Staying in unhealthy or unfulfilling relationships due to an intense fear of being alone or abandoned.
- Difficulty Expressing Disagreements: Avoiding conflicts or suppressing one's views to keep the peace or satisfy the other person.

The Impact of Co-dependency

Co-dependency not only perpetuates anxious attachment behaviors but also leads to a host of emotional and relational issues. It can result in diminished self-esteem, loss of personal identity, and chronic dissatisfaction within relationships. Moreover, co-dependent dynamics often hinder personal growth and the development of healthy coping mechanisms, making it difficult for individuals to function independently or maintain equal, mutually satisfying relationships.

Relationship sabotage

An integral facet of the journey toward recovering from anxious attachment involves confronting and overcoming the propensity for relationship sabotage. Individuals grappling with anxious attachment often find themselves in a paradoxical struggle: deeply craving intimacy and closeness while simultaneously engaging in behaviors that push others away. This chapter delves into the complexities of relationship sabotage within the context of anxious attachment, illuminating the underlying mechanisms at play and offering strategies for breaking free from these self-defeating patterns.

Understanding Relationship Sabotage

Relationship sabotage can manifest in various forms, from constant criticism and jealousy to excessive clinginess and unreasonable demands for reassurance. This sabotage stems from deep-seated fears and insecurities about one's worthiness of love and the relationship's stability. For those with an anxious attachment style, these fears are magnified, leading to behaviors that inadvertently undermine the very connections they long to preserve.

The cycle of relationship sabotage often begins with anxiety triggered by perceived threats to the relationship, such as a partner's independence or attention to others. This anxiety activates defense mechanisms designed to protect the individual from anticipated pain, such as rejection or abandonment. However, these protective behaviors—whether withdrawal, aggression, or control—tend to alienate partners, increasing the likelihood of the outcomes they aim to prevent.

Whether intentional or unconscious, relationship sabotage can have profound and lasting effects on both the partnership and the individuals involved; understanding the dangers associated with sabotage can help recognize the urgency of addressing these behaviors. Here are some of the critical risks associated with relationship sabotage:

Erosion of Trust

One of the most immediate dangers of sabotage is the erosion of trust between partners. Behaviors such as lying, infidelity, or consistent unreliability can severely damage the foundation of trust that relationships need to thrive. Once trust is broken, rebuilding can be challenging, leading to ongoing suspicion and insecurity.

The erosion of trust within a relationship occurs gradually over time and can have significant consequences for the health and stability of the partnership. Trust is the foundation of a solid and fulfilling relationship, and its erosion can lead to feelings of insecurity, resentment, and emotional distance. Here's how the erosion of trust may manifest and some strategies for rebuilding trust:

Signs of Erosion of Trust:

Lack of Communication: Communication breakdowns, avoidance of difficult conversations, or withholding information can indicate a lack of trust within the relationship.

Secretiveness: Keeping secrets or being overly secretive about activities, interactions, or personal matters can undermine trust and foster suspicion.

Broken Promises: Repeatedly breaking promises, commitments, or agreements can erode trust and create feelings of disappointment and betrayal.

Deception: Dishonesty, lying, or deception about essential matters can damage trust and lead to betrayal and disillusionment.

Inconsistency: Inconsistent behavior, mood swings, or changes in patterns of interaction may signal underlying issues that undermine trust.

Jealousy and Suspicion: Excessive jealousy, suspicion, or insecurity within the relationship can indicate a lack of trust and foster a toxic environment of mistrust.

Emotional Distress

Sabotage can lead to significant emotional distress for both partners. The partner on the receiving end of sabotage may experience confusion, betrayal, sadness, and anger. For the partner engaging in sabotage, underlying issues such as fear of intimacy or low self-esteem can contribute to feelings of guilt, shame, and self-loathing. This emotional turmoil can exacerbate mental health issues, including anxiety and depression.

Emotional distress refers to a range of uncomfortable or painful emotions that individuals experience in response to challenging life events, stressors, or internal conflicts. It encompasses feelings such as sadness, anxiety, anger, fear, guilt, shame, loneliness, and despair. Emotional distress can vary in intensity and duration, from temporary feelings of discomfort to overwhelming and persistent emotional pain.

Causes of Emotional Distress:

Life Events: Significant life events such as the loss of a loved one, relationship problems, job loss, financial difficulties, illness, or trauma can trigger emotional distress.

Stressors: Everyday stressors such as work pressure, academic demands, family conflicts, or significant life transitions can contribute to feelings of emotional distress.

Unresolved Emotions: Suppressed or unprocessed emotions, unresolved conflicts, or past traumas can resurface and contribute to emotional distress.

Internal Factors: Personal factors such as low self-esteem, perfectionism, negative self-talk, excessive worry, or rumination can exacerbate emotional distress.

Biological Factors: Biological factors such as genetics, brain chemistry, hormonal imbalances, or medical conditions may play a role in predisposing individuals to emotional distress.

Signs and Symptoms of Emotional Distress:

Mood Changes: Fluctuations in mood, such as feeling sad, anxious, irritable, or numb, may indicate emotional distress.

Physical Symptoms: Physical manifestations of emotional distress can include headaches, muscle tension, fatigue, gastrointestinal problems, changes in appetite or sleep patterns, and increased susceptibility to illness.

Cognitive Symptoms: Cognitive symptoms may include racing thoughts, difficulty concentrating, memory problems, negative self-talk, or intrusive thoughts.

Behavioral Changes: Changes in behavior such as social withdrawal, avoidance of activities or responsibilities, increased use of substances, or self-destructive behaviors may indicate emotional distress.

Interpersonal Difficulties: Difficulties in relationships, conflict with others, or feelings of loneliness and isolation may be signs of emotional distress.

By acknowledging and addressing emotional distress in healthy and adaptive ways, individuals can cultivate resilience, self-awareness, and emotional well-being, ultimately enhancing their ability to cope with life's challenges and thrive in adversity.

Cycle of Negative Interactions

Sabotage can create a cycle of negative interactions where defensive behaviors, arguments, and misunderstandings become the norm. This cycle can stifle positive communication, intimacy, and growth, making it more challenging for the relationship to recover and progress.

Loss of Intimacy and Connection

Intimacy and connection are vital for a healthy relationship. Sabotage behaviors can create a barrier to these elements, leading to a sense of loneliness and disconnection within the partnership. Over time, this can diminish the emotional and physical closeness necessary for a fulfilling relationship.

Impact on Self-Esteem and Identity

Being in a relationship marked by sabotage can negatively impact individuals' self-esteem and sense of self. The partner experiencing sabotage may begin to question their worth and value, leading to diminished self-esteem. Similarly, the partner engaging in sabotage might struggle with feelings of inadequacy and unworthiness, further entrenching unhealthy behaviors.

Physical Health Consequences

The stress and emotional turmoil associated with relationship sabotage can have direct impacts on physical health. Stress-related symptoms such as headaches, insomnia, high blood pressure, and a weakened immune system can arise. Additionally, emotional distress can lead to unhealthy coping mechanisms, such as substance abuse or neglect of physical health.

Disruption of Social and Family Dynamics

Relationship sabotage can extend beyond the couple, affecting family and social dynamics. Conflicts may spill over into interactions with children, relatives, and mutual friends, leading to wider circles of stress and discord. This can disrupt family harmony and social relationships, isolating the couple further.

Long-term Relational Damage

In the absence of intervention and genuine efforts to change, sabotage can lead to long-term damage that may be irreparable. Relationships can reach a point where the accumulated hurt and distrust are too overwhelming to overcome, leading to separation or divorce.

Preventing Personal Growth

Sabotage can prevent both partners from achieving personal growth and fulfillment. The energy consumed by navigating the relationship's challenges can divert attention from personal ambitions, self-improvement, and pursuing individual passions.

Recognizing and addressing sabotage early is crucial to preventing these dangers and fostering a healthy, supportive relationship. Both partners must be willing to work on underlying issues, communicate openly, and seek professional help if necessary. With commitment and effort, overcoming sabotage and rebuilding a stronger, more secure partnership is possible.

Breaking the Cycle of Sabotage

Cultivating Self-Awareness

The first step in overcoming relationship sabotage is developing a keen awareness of one's patterns and triggers. Recognizing how anxious attachment influences perceptions and behaviors allows individuals to pause and choose different responses. Journaling, mindfulness practices, and reflective therapy can facilitate this self-awareness.

Enhancing Communication Skills

Open, honest, and vulnerable communication is essential for addressing the fears and needs underlying sabotaging behaviors. Learning to express oneself clearly and constructively, without accusation or defensiveness, can help de-escalate conflicts and foster understanding and intimacy.

Building Trust in Relationships

Trust is the antidote to fear. Building trust involves trusting partners, oneself, and the resilience of the relationship. This trust can be cultivated through consistent, reliable actions and responses, gradually reducing the perceived need for sabotage as a defense mechanism.

Seeking Professional Help

Therapy can be a powerful tool in unraveling the complex dynamics of relationship sabotage. Therapists specializing in attachment and relational issues can offer insights, coping strategies, and a safe space to explore and heal the underlying wounds driving sabotaging behaviors.

Fostering Independence and Self-Sufficiency

Anxious attachment often leads to overdependence on partners for emotional fulfillment and self-esteem. Cultivating independence and self-sufficiency—through personal interests, social connections, and self-care practices—can mitigate the fear of abandonment and reduce the impulse to sabotage.

Practicing Patience and Compassion

Recovery from anxious attachment and the tendency to sabotage relationships is a process that requires patience and compassion. Mistakes and setbacks are inevitable, but they offer valuable lessons and opportunities for growth. Treating oneself with kindness and understanding through this journey is crucial.

The path to overcoming relationship sabotage in the context of anxious attachment recovery is both challenging and profoundly rewarding. It requires courage to confront deep-seated fears, commitment to personal growth, and openness to changing long-standing behavior patterns. By addressing the root causes of sabotage and employing strategies to foster healthier relationship dynamics, individuals can move towards creating the secure, loving connections they desire. This journey transforms relationships and promotes a deeper, more compassionate relationship with oneself, marking a pivotal step toward healing and fulfillment.

When your partner engages in relationship sabotage, it can be challenging and disheartening, especially if you're committed to building a healthy and supportive relationship. Relationship sabotage can manifest in various ways, such as withdrawal, jealousy, criticism, or creating unnecessary conflict. Addressing this behavior requires patience, understanding, and a strategic approach. Here are steps you can take to navigate this situation effectively:

1. Recognize the Signs of Sabotage

First, it's crucial to identify behaviors that signify sabotage. These might include unnecessary arguments, reluctance to discuss the future, creating distance, or undermining trust. Understanding these signs can help you approach the situation with clarity.

2. Communicate Openly and Honestly

Open and honest communication is vital. Express your observations and concerns without blame or judgment. Use "I" statements to describe how their behavior affects you and the relationship. Encourage your partner to share their feelings and fears that might drive their actions.

3. Practice Active Listening

Listen actively to your partner's concerns and feelings when discussing sabotage issues. Validate their emotions without immediately trying to solve the problem. This validation can foster a safe environment for honest dialogue.

4. Encourage Self-awareness

Encourage your partner to reflect on their behaviors and how they might stem from deeper insecurities or fears. Self-awareness is the first step toward change. I suggest journaling or engaging in reflective practices to explore underlying issues.

5. Seek to Understand Attachment Styles

Understanding your and your partner's attachment styles can provide valuable insights into relationship dynamics. If sabotage stems from an anxious or avoidant attachment style, recognizing this can guide your approach to healing.

6. Promote Professional Support

Sometimes, professional help is necessary to overcome deeply ingrained patterns of sabotage. Encourage your partner to consider therapy, either individually or as a couple. A therapist can offer strategies and support to address the root causes of sabotaging behaviors.

7. Set Boundaries

While supporting your partner, setting and maintaining healthy boundaries is essential. Communicate your needs and limits. Boundaries are crucial for your well-being and for establishing respect in the relationship.

8. Foster Independence and Self-growth

Encourage your partner (and yourself) to pursue individual interests, hobbies, and friendships. Independence within the relationship can alleviate pressures contributing to sabotage, fostering a healthier dynamic.

9. Reinforce Positive Behaviors

Acknowledge and appreciate the efforts your partner makes toward positive change. Positive reinforcement can motivate further growth and reduce sabotaging behaviors.

10. Practice Patience and Compassion

Remember that change takes time. Be patient with your partner's progress and with your reactions. Compassion for yourself and your partner during this process is crucial.

11. Evaluate the Relationship

While working through sabotage, continually evaluate the health and progress of the relationship. Consider whether both partners are committed to improvement and if the relationship is moving toward a healthier state.

Addressing relationship sabotage is a delicate process that requires mutual effort, understanding, and patience. It's about balancing support for your partner with maintaining your emotional health. If both partners are committed to overcoming these challenges, building a stronger, more fulfilling relationship is possible.

Part IV

Strategies for Overcoming Anxious Attachment

Recovering from anxious attachment and cultivating secure attachment patterns is a transformative journey that requires introspection, understanding, and active engagement in new relational behaviors. Secure attachment, characterized by comfort with closeness and independence, trust in relationship stability, and effective communication, is attainable even for those who have navigated the tumultuous waters of anxious attachment. This chapter delves into strategies and insights for developing secure attachment patterns, offering a beacon of hope for individuals seeking healthier, more fulfilling relationships.

Understanding the Foundation of Secure Attachment

Secure attachment is rooted in consistency, reliability, and emotional availability. It allows individuals to feel safe expressing their needs and vulnerabilities, confident they will be met with understanding and support. Developing secure attachment patterns involves rewiring long-held beliefs and behaviors, a process that, while challenging, is rich with rewards.

Recognizing Anxious Patterns

The first step in cultivating secure attachment is recognizing the signs of anxious attachment within oneself. This may manifest as fear of abandonment, excessive need for reassurance, and difficulty trusting partners. By acknowledging these patterns, individuals can begin to understand their origins—often in early childhood experiences—and how they influence current relationships.

Fostering Self-awareness and Self-compassion

Developing secure attachment requires a deep dive into self-awareness. Understanding one's emotions, triggers, and relationship behaviors allows for conscious navigation of attachment-related challenges. Self-compassion is crucial in this process; healing is not linear, and treating oneself with kindness and understanding fosters resilience and growth.

Building Emotional Regulation Skills

At the heart of anxious attachment lies a struggle with emotional regulation. Cultivating mindfulness, deep breathing, and positive self-talk can enhance emotional resilience. These practices help individuals manage anxiety and fear more effectively, reducing the impulse to react in ways that undermine relationship security.

Establishing Healthy Boundaries

Secure attachment thrives on healthy boundaries—communicated limits that respect both partners' needs, independence, and individuality. Setting and maintaining boundaries is essential for mitigating codependency and fostering mutual respect and understanding in relationships.

Enhancing Communication

Effective communication is a cornerstone of secure attachment. This involves expressing needs, desires, and concerns openly, constructively, and actively listening to and validating one's partner. Developing these communication skills can prevent misunderstandings and build trust and intimacy.

Seeking and Providing Consistent Support

Reliability and predictability in providing emotional support reinforce secure attachment. This includes being present for one's partner during times of need and seeking support in a healthy, balanced manner. Consistency in these actions builds trust, demonstrating that both partners can depend on each other.

Embracing Vulnerability

Vulnerability is integral to developing deep, secure connections. It involves opening up about fears, hopes, and dreams and allowing oneself to be seen fully. While vulnerability can be daunting, especially for those with anxious attachment, it is through this openness that true intimacy and security are cultivated.

Pursuing Individual Growth and Independence

A hallmark of secure attachment is the balance between closeness and independence. Encouraging personal growth and supporting each other's pursuits strengthens the relationship by fostering mutual admiration and respect.

Engaging in Continuous Relationship Work

Secure attachment is not a destination but a continuous journey of growth and adaptation. Regularly investing time and effort into the relationship through shared experiences, ongoing communication, and mutual support keeps the bond strong and resilient.

Seeking Professional Guidance

For many, the journey from anxiety to secure attachment benefits from professional guidance. Therapy can offer personalized strategies, support, and insights into overcoming attachment-related challenges, facilitating more profound understanding and growth.

Developing secure attachment patterns is a profound journey of transformation that promises more prosperous, more fulfilling relationships. By engaging in self-reflection, building emotional regulation skills, establishing healthy boundaries, and fostering open communication, individuals can move beyond the constraints of anxious attachment. Embracing vulnerability, pursuing personal growth, and committing to continuous relationship work further solidifies secure attachment's foundations. With patience, perseverance, and professional support, transitioning from anxious to secure attachment enhances relational dynamics and fosters a more profound sense of personal peace and satisfaction.

Emulating secure attachment behaviors

Emulating secure attachment behaviors involves adopting and practicing relational patterns and behaviors that mirror certain attachment relationships. Secure attachment is characterized by trust, emotional responsiveness, and a sense of relationship safety and security. Emulating these behaviors can help individuals foster healthier connections with others and cultivate greater emotional well-being. Here's how to emulate secure attachment behaviors:

1. Developing Emotional Awareness:

Please recognize your emotions and learn to identify and label them accurately. Practice mindfulness techniques to increase your awareness of your emotional experiences in the present moment.

2. Being Present and Attentive:

Practice active listening when interacting with others, giving them your full attention and showing genuine interest in what they say.

Be physically and emotionally present in your interactions, demonstrating reliability and responsiveness.

3. Expressing Empathy and Understanding:

Show empathy and understanding towards others by acknowledging their feelings and validating their experiences.

Practice perspective-taking to understand things from the other person's point of view, even if you disagree with them.

4. Setting Boundaries and Consistency:

Establish clear and healthy boundaries in your relationships, communicating your needs and respecting the boundaries of others.

Be consistent in your words and actions, creating a sense of predictability and stability in your interactions.

5. Providing Support and Comfort:

Offer support and comfort to others during times of distress or difficulty, demonstrating that you are available and reliable as a source of assistance.

Validate their emotions and reassure them of your presence and willingness to help.

6. Fostering Trust and Security:

Build trust in your relationships by being honest, reliable, and trustworthy in your interactions.

Create a safe and secure environment where others feel comfortable expressing themselves and being vulnerable.

7. Communicating Effectively:

Practice open and honest communication, expressing yourself clearly and respectfully.

Encourage open dialogue and feedback in your relationships, fostering mutual understanding and collaboration.

8. Repairing Relationship Strains:

Constructively address conflicts or misunderstandings, focusing on finding solutions and repairing the relationship rather than assigning blame.

Apologize sincerely when necessary and make efforts to rebuild trust and connection.

9. Seeking Support and Self-Care:

Prioritize your emotional well-being by seeking support from trusted friends, family members, or mental health professionals when needed.

Practice self-care activities that promote relaxation, stress reduction, and emotional regulation.

By consciously emulating these secure attachment behaviors in your relationships, you can create a positive and supportive interpersonal environment that fosters emotional security, intimacy, and resilience.

Emulating secure attachment involves adopting behaviors and attitudes that promote trust, emotional connection, and security in relationships.

Emulating Secure Attachment in a Romantic Relationship

1. Communication and Emotional Expressiveness:

Express Feelings: Share your feelings openly and honestly with your partner. Practice expressing emotions healthily and constructively.

Active Listening: Listen actively to your partner's thoughts and feelings without judgment or defensiveness. Show empathy and understanding.

2. Building Trust and Reliability:

Consistency: Be consistent in your actions and words. Follow through on your commitments and promises.

Transparency: Be open and transparent with your partner. Avoid keeping secrets or hiding significant information.

3. Providing Support and Comfort:

Offer Support: Be there for your partner during challenging times. Offer emotional support, encouragement, and practical assistance as needed.

Comfort: Provide comfort and reassurance when your partner is anxious or upset. Offer hugs, affectionate gestures, or comforting words.

4. Respecting Boundaries and Autonomy:

Respect Boundaries: Respect your partner's boundaries and personal space. Avoid pressuring them into doing things they're not comfortable with.

Encourage Independence: Support your partner's goals, interests, and autonomy. Please encourage them to pursue their passions and individual growth.

5. Conflict Resolution and Repair:

Healthy Conflict Resolution: Approach conflicts with a willingness to listen, compromise, and find solutions. Avoid blame or criticism.

Repairing Relationship Strains: Apologize when you make mistakes or hurt your partner unintentionally. Make efforts to improve the relationship and rebuild trust.

6. Creating Emotional Safety:

Nonjudgmental Atmosphere: Foster an environment where your partner feels safe to express themselves without fear of judgment or rejection.

Emotional Availability: Be emotionally available and responsive to your partner's needs, even during stress or disagreement.

7. Celebrating Successes and Milestones:

Celebrate Together: Celebrate your partner's successes, achievements, and milestones. Show genuine happiness and pride in their accomplishments.

Share Joy: Share joyful moments and experiences, strengthening your emotional bond and connection.

8. Nurturing Intimacy and Affection:

Physical Affection: Show physical affection regularly through hugs, kisses, cuddling, and other gestures of intimacy.

Emotional Intimacy: Foster emotional intimacy by sharing your thoughts, fears, dreams, and vulnerabilities with your partner. Create a deep emotional connection.

9. Prioritizing the Relationship:

Quality Time: Make time for each other regularly, whether through date nights, shared activities, or simply spending quality time together.

Investment: Invest time, effort, and energy into nurturing and strengthening your relationship. Prioritize your partnership as a central aspect of your life.

By consistently practicing these behaviors and attitudes, you can emulate secure attachment in your romantic relationship, fostering a deep trust, emotional connection, and security between you and your partner.

The role of therapy and support groups

Therapy and support groups play vital roles in helping individuals address various mental health concerns, cope with life challenges, and develop healthier coping strategies and relationships. Here's an overview of their roles:

Therapy:

1. Individualized Treatment:

Therapy provides personalized treatment tailored to the individual's needs, preferences, and goals.

A therapist works collaboratively with the client to explore their thoughts, emotions and behaviors and develop effective strategies for managing them.

2. Emotional Support:

Therapists offer a safe and supportive environment where clients can express themselves freely and explore complex emotions without fear of judgment.

Through empathetic listening and validation, therapists help clients feel understood and accepted, which can be healing.

3. Skill Building:

Therapy equips individuals with practical skills and techniques to cope with stress, regulate emotions, improve communication, and navigate life's challenges more effectively.

Cognitive-behavioral, dialectical behavior, mindfulness-based, and other evidence-based therapies offer structured approaches to skill-building.

4. Insight and Self-Exploration:

Therapy facilitates self-exploration and introspection, helping individuals gain insight into their thoughts, feelings, and behaviors.

By uncovering underlying patterns and motivations, clients can better understand themselves and their relationships.

5. Crisis Intervention:

Therapists provide crisis intervention and support during times of acute distress or mental health crises, helping clients manage overwhelming emotions and stay safe.

Crisis intervention techniques may include safety planning, relaxation exercises, and connecting clients with additional support services.

Support Groups:

1. Peer Support:

Support groups offer a sense of belonging and connection through shared experiences with others facing similar challenges.

Peer support can reduce feelings of isolation and stigma, providing validation and empathy from individuals who understand firsthand what it's like to cope with a particular issue.

2. Shared Learning and Coping Strategies:

Participants in support groups share practical tips, coping strategies, and resources for managing symptoms and improving well-being.

Learning from others' experiences can offer new perspectives and insights, empowering individuals to explore different approaches to their challenges.

3. Normalization of Experiences:

Support groups help normalize individuals' experiences by demonstrating that they are not alone in their struggles.

Hearing others' stories and successes can instill hope and optimism, reminding participants that recovery and growth are possible.

4. Encouragement and Motivation:

Support groups provide encouragement, motivation, and accountability as participants work towards their goals.

Sharing progress, setbacks, and achievements in a supportive environment can boost self-esteem and resilience.

5. Community and Social Connection:

Support groups foster a sense of community and social connection, offering opportunities for friendship, camaraderie, and mutual support beyond the group setting.

Building relationships with peers who share everyday experiences can enhance social support networks and promote overall well-being.

Therapy and support groups offer complementary approaches to mental health support, providing individualized treatment, emotional support, skill-building, and a sense of community. Whether seeking professional guidance from a therapist or connecting with peers in a support group, individuals can find valuable resources and encouragement to navigate their mental health journey and cultivate greater resilience and well-being.

Self-Healing and Personal Development

Self-healing and personal development are processes through which individuals strive to address emotional wounds, cultivate resilience, and enhance their overall well-being. These processes involve various strategies, techniques, and practices to foster self-awareness, growth, and transformation. Here's an overview:

Self-Healing:

1. Self-Awareness:

Self-healing begins with self-awareness, the ability to recognize and understand one's thoughts, emotions, and behaviors.

Individuals can begin healing emotional wounds and traumas by acknowledging and accepting inner experiences without judgment.

2. Emotional Processing:

Self-healing involves exploring and processing emotions, including painful or suppressed feelings.

Techniques like journaling, mindfulness, and expressive arts therapy can help individuals safely explore and release pent-up emotions.

3. Self-Compassion:

Cultivating self-compassion is crucial for self-healing, as it involves treating oneself with kindness, understanding, and empathy.

Practicing self-compassion involves acknowledging one's suffering without self-criticism and offering oneself the same care and Support as one would offer a loved one.

4. Boundaries and Self-Care:

Establishing healthy boundaries is essential for self-healing, as it involves prioritizing one's needs and well-being.

Practicing self-care involves engaging in activities and practices that nourish and rejuvenate the mind, body, and spirit, such as exercise, relaxation techniques, and hobbies.

5. Forgiveness and Letting Go:

Forgiveness is a crucial aspect of self-healing, as it involves releasing resentment, anger, and bitterness towards oneself or others.

Letting go of past hurts and grievances allows individuals to move forward with greater peace and emotional freedom.

6. Seeking Support:

While self-healing is an individual journey, seeking support from trusted friends, family members, or mental health professionals can be beneficial.

Therapy, support groups, and mentorship provide valuable resources and guidance for individuals navigating their healing journey.

Personal Development:

1. Goal Setting:

Personal development involves setting meaningful goals and aspirations for oneself, whether related to career advancement, skill acquisition, or personal growth.

Setting SMART goals (Specific, Measurable, Achievable, Relevant, Time-bound) provides a framework for effective goal-setting.

2. Continuous Learning:

Personal development entails a commitment to lifelong learning and growth.

Individuals engage in formal education, self-study, workshops, seminars, and other learning opportunities to expand their knowledge and skills.

3. Self-Reflection and Evaluation:

Personal development requires regular self-reflection and evaluation of one's strengths, weaknesses, and areas for improvement.

Techniques such as journaling, meditation, and feedback from others facilitate self-awareness and personal growth.

4. Skill Building:

Personal development involves developing and honing skills relevant to personal and professional goals.

Individuals seek opportunities to acquire new skills, improve existing ones, and stay abreast of industry trends and advancements.

5. Adaptability and Resilience:

Personal development fosters adaptability and resilience in the face of challenges and setbacks.

Individuals cultivate a growth mindset, viewing obstacles as opportunities for learning and development rather than insurmountable barriers.

6. Purpose and Meaning:

A sense of purpose and meaning drives personal development as individuals strive to align their actions and goals with their values and passions.

Clarifying one's purpose and values provides direction and motivation for personal growth and fulfillment.

Self-healing and personal development are interconnected processes that empower individuals to overcome past traumas, cultivate resilience, and strive toward greater fulfillment and growth. By embracing self-awareness, self-compassion, goal setting, continuous learning, and other strategies, individuals can embark on transformative journeys of healing, discovery, and personal evolution.

Mindfulness and self-awareness practices

Mindfulness and self-awareness practices cultivate present-moment awareness, attention, and non-judgmental observation of one's thoughts, emotions, and sensations. These practices help individuals develop greater clarity, insight, and understanding of themselves and their inner experiences. Here's an overview along with an example practice:

Mindfulness:

1. Definition:

Mindfulness involves paying deliberate attention to the present moment with openness, curiosity, and acceptance.

It involves observing thoughts, emotions, bodily sensations, and the surrounding environment without judgment.

2. Benefits:

Reduces stress, anxiety, and rumination.

Enhances emotional regulation and resilience.

Improves focus, concentration, and cognitive function.

Fosters greater self-awareness and compassion.

3. Practices:

Breath Awareness: Focus on the sensation of your breath as it enters and leaves your body. Notice the rise and fall of your chest or the feeling of air passing through your nostrils.

Body Scan: Slowly and systematically scan your body from head to toe, noticing any areas of tension, discomfort, or sensation. Bring gentle awareness to each part of your body without trying to change anything.

Mindful Eating: Eat slowly and attentively, savoring each bite and noticing the taste, texture, and sensations of the food. Pay attention to the act of chewing, swallowing, and the feeling of nourishment in your body.

Walking Meditation: Take a leisurely walk while paying attention to each step and the sensations of walking—the feeling of your feet making contact with the ground, the movement of your legs, and the rhythm of your breath.

Self-Awareness Practices:

1. Definition:

Self-awareness involves clearly understanding one's thoughts, emotions, motivations, strengths, weaknesses, and values.

It enables individuals to recognize how their inner experiences influence their behavior and relationships.

2. Benefits:

Enhances emotional intelligence and self-regulation.

Facilitates personal growth, self-acceptance, and authenticity.

Improves decision-making and interpersonal communication.

Strengthens resilience and adaptive coping skills.

3. Practices:

Journaling: Set aside time daily to write about your thoughts, feelings, and experiences. Reflect on your successes, challenges, and areas for growth.

Self-Reflection: Take regular breaks to pause and reflect on your thoughts, emotions, and behaviors. Ask yourself questions, "What am I feeling right now?" or "What are my underlying motivations?"

Mindful Observation: Observe yourself in various situations without judgment or reaction. Notice how you react to stimuli, triggers, or stressors, and explore the underlying patterns and beliefs driving your responses.

Feedback Seeking: Seek feedback from trusted friends, mentors, or colleagues about your strengths, weaknesses, and blind spots. Listen openly and non-defensively to their perspectives, and use their insights to deepen your self-awareness.

Example Practice: Mindful Breathing

Steps:

Find a quiet and comfortable space where you won't be disturbed for a few minutes.

Sit or lie down in a relaxed position, with your back straight but not rigid.

Close your eyes or keep them softly focused on a point before you.

Take a few deep breaths, inhaling slowly through your nose and exhaling through your mouth to release tension.

Allow your breath to return to its natural rhythm.

Bring your attention to the sensation of your breath as it enters and leaves your body.

Notice the rising and falling of your chest or abdomen with each inhale and exhale.

If your mind wanders, gently bring your focus back to your breath without judgment or frustration.

Continue to breathe mindfully for a few minutes, observing each breath with curiosity and openness.

When you're ready, gradually bring your awareness back to your surroundings and gently open your eyes.

By practicing mindfulness and self-awareness regularly, individuals can cultivate more significant presence, clarity, and insight into their inner experiences, enhancing well-being and personal growth.

Building self-esteem and independence

Building self-esteem and independence are essential aspects of personal development that contribute to a sense of confidence, self-worth, and autonomy.

Building Self-Esteem:

Self-esteem refers to the overall subjective evaluation of one's own worth, value, and capabilities.

It involves having a positive self-image, self-respect, and confidence in one's abilities.

Greater resilience in the face of challenges and setbacks.

Improved mental health and well-being.

More fulfilling relationships and social interactions.

Increased motivation and achievement in pursuing goals.

Positive Self-Talk: Challenge negative self-talk and replace it with affirming and encouraging statements. Focus on your strengths, accomplishments, and potential.

Set Realistic Goals: Set achievable goals that align with your interests, values, and abilities. Celebrate your progress and accomplishments along the way.

Practice Self-Compassion: Treat yourself with kindness, understanding, and acceptance, especially during difficult times. Acknowledge that everyone makes mistakes and experiences setbacks.

Engage in Activities You Enjoy: Pursue hobbies, interests, and activities that bring you joy and fulfillment. Engaging in enjoyable activities boosts self-esteem and enhances overall well-being.

Surround Yourself with Supportive People: Seek out relationships with individuals who uplift and support you. Surrounding yourself with positive influences reinforces feelings of self-worth and validation.

Building Independence:

Independence involves the ability to think, act, and make decisions autonomously, without excessive reliance on others.

It encompasses self-reliance, self-sufficiency, and the capacity to meet one's own needs.

Increased confidence and self-trust.

Greater sense of empowerment and control over one's life.

Enhanced problem-solving and decision-making skills.

Improved adaptability and resilience in navigating life's challenges.

Take Initiative: Proactively take steps to pursue your goals and desires. Initiate actions and make decisions independently, rather than waiting for others to take the lead.

Develop Practical Skills: Cultivate practical skills and competencies that enhance your ability to meet your own needs and navigate daily life effectively. This may include cooking, budgeting, time management, and organization.

Set Boundaries: Establish clear boundaries in your relationships and interactions with others. Advocate for your needs and preferences while respecting the boundaries of others.

Seek Knowledge and Resources: Take initiative in seeking out information, resources, and support that can help you achieve your goals and solve problems independently. Utilize libraries, online resources, and community services.

Embrace Challenges: Embrace challenges and obstacles as opportunities for growth and learning. Approach new experiences with a willingness to learn from mistakes and setbacks.

Setting Boundaries in Relationships

Scenario: You have a friend who often asks you for favors or assistance, but you find that it sometimes interferes with your own priorities and responsibilities.

Example of Building Self-Esteem: Practice positive self-talk by reminding yourself of your own worth and the importance of prioritizing your needs and boundaries. Affirm your right to assert yourself and set boundaries in relationships.

Example of Building Independence: Take initiative in setting clear boundaries with your friend by politely but assertively communicating your limits and expectations. Explain that while you value your friendship, you need to prioritize your own commitments and may not always be available to help.

Outcome: By setting boundaries and advocating for your needs, you reinforce feelings of self-worth and autonomy. Additionally, you cultivate a healthier, more balanced relationship dynamic based on mutual respect and understanding.

Strategies for Enhancing Emotional Regulation

Developing Awareness

The first step towards better emotional regulation is developing a deeper awareness of one's emotions and triggers. Mindfulness practices can be particularly effective in cultivating this awareness, enabling individuals to observe their emotional responses without immediate reaction.

Cognitive-Behavioral Techniques

Cognitive-behavioral strategies (CBT) can help individuals challenge and reframe the negative thought patterns that often underlie emotional dysregulation. By identifying and altering these thoughts, it becomes possible to change emotional responses and behavioral reactions. Here's an example of a cognitive-behavioral technique called "Thought Record":

Thought Record

Step 1: Identifying the Situation

Identify a specific situation that caused distress or negative emotions. For example, feeling anxious before giving a presentation at work.

Step 2: Identifying Automatic Thoughts

Write down the automatic thoughts that came to mind during that situation. These are often quick, reflexive thoughts that may not be rational or helpful. For example, "I'm going to mess up and embarrass myself."

Step 3: Evaluating Thoughts

Evaluate the accuracy and helpfulness of each automatic thought. Ask yourself questions like:

- Is there evidence that supports or contradicts this thought?
- Is this thought based on facts or assumptions?
- Would someone else in the same situation think the same way?

Step 4: Generating Alternative Thoughts

Generate alternative, more balanced thoughts that are based on evidence and are more realistic. For example:

- "I've prepared thoroughly for this presentation, and I know my material."
- "Even if I make a mistake, it's not the end of the world. Everyone makes mistakes."

Step 5: Re-evaluating Emotions

Re-evaluate your emotions after considering the alternative thoughts. Notice any changes in how you feel and rate the intensity of your distress on a scale from 0 to 100.

Step 6: Behavior Change

Consider how adopting these alternative thoughts might change your behavior. For example, feeling more confident and prepared might lead you to approach the presentation with a calmer demeanor.

Step 7: Practice and Repeat

Practice this process regularly, especially in situations where you experience distressing thoughts or emotions. Over time, you'll become more adept at identifying and challenging negative thought patterns.

Building a Secure Base

Establishing secure and supportive relationships can provide a foundation for practicing and improving emotional regulation. These relationships can offer a safe space for expressing emotions, receiving validation, and learning new coping mechanisms.

Example: Parent-Child Relationship

1. Responsive Caregiving:

- Emotional Availability: Be emotionally available and responsive to the child's needs, including physical comfort, soothing, and affection.
- Consistency: Establish consistent routines and responses, providing a sense of predictability and safety.

2. Creating a Safe Environment:

- Physical Safety: Ensure the child's physical environment is safe and free from harm.
- Emotional Safety: Foster an emotionally safe environment where the child feels free to express themselves without fear of judgment or rejection.

3. Attunement and Empathy:

- Active Listening: Practice active listening, attuning to the child's verbal and nonverbal cues to understand their emotions and experiences.
- Empathetic Responses: Respond with empathy and validation, acknowledging the child's feelings and experiences.

4. Promoting Exploration and Autonomy:

- Encouragement: Encourage the child to explore their environment and develop autonomy, providing support and guidance when needed.
- Independence: Allow the child to make age-appropriate decisions and take on responsibilities, fostering a sense of competence and self-efficacy.

5. Maintaining Secure Attachments:

- Consistent Presence: Be physically and emotionally present for the child, establishing a secure attachment bond characterized by trust and mutual affection.
- Attending to Separation: Acknowledge and support the child's emotions during separations, reassuring them of your continued presence and availability.

6. Repairing Relationship Strains:

- Conflict Resolution: Address conflicts or misunderstandings in a constructive manner, modeling effective communication and problem-solving skills.
- Apologizing and Reconnecting: When mistakes occur, apologize sincerely and make efforts to repair the relationship, reaffirming your commitment to the child's well-being.

7. Modeling Secure Relationships:

- Healthy Relationships: Model healthy interpersonal relationships and emotional regulation, demonstrating empathy, respect, and trust in your interactions with others.
- Self-Care: Prioritize self-care and stress management, demonstrating the importance of self-nurturance and emotional well-being.

By following these practices consistently, caregivers can provide a secure base from which children can explore the world, develop healthy relationships, and navigate life's challenges with confidence and resilience.

Emotional Regulation Skills

Specific skills, such as deep breathing, progressive muscle relaxation, and positive imagery, can be effective tools for managing acute emotional distress. Over time, these practices can help reduce the intensity and duration of emotional responses.

Example: Deep Breathing Exercise

1. Find a Comfortable Position:

Sit or lie down in a comfortable position. Close your eyes if it helps you focus.

2. Focus on Your Breath:

Take a few moments to focus your attention on your breath. Notice the sensation of air entering and leaving your body.

3. Diaphragmatic Breathing:

Place one hand on your chest and the other on your abdomen.

Inhale slowly and deeply through your nose, allowing your abdomen to rise as you fill your lungs with air. Feel your hand on your abdomen move outward.

Exhale slowly and completely through your mouth, allowing your abdomen to fall as you release the air. Feel your hand on your abdomen move inward.

Repeat this deep breathing pattern several times, focusing on the rise and fall of your abdomen with each breath.

4. Counting Breaths:

To enhance focus, you can count your breaths. Inhale slowly to the count of four, hold your breath for a moment, and then exhale slowly to the count of six or eight.

Adjust the counting to a rhythm that feels comfortable and calming for you.

5. Body Scan:

As you continue to breathe deeply, scan your body for any areas of tension or discomfort.

With each exhale, imagine releasing tension from these areas, allowing your muscles to relax and soften.

6. Notice Thoughts and Emotions:

While practicing deep breathing, you may notice thoughts or emotions arising. Acknowledge them without judgment and gently redirect your focus back to your breath.

7. Practice Regularly:

Set aside time each day to practice deep breathing exercises, especially during moments of stress or heightened emotions.

With consistent practice, deep breathing can become a powerful tool for calming your mind and regulating your emotions in various situations.

8. Integration into Daily Life:

Once you feel comfortable with deep breathing, integrate it into your daily life as a proactive strategy for managing stress and promoting emotional well-being.

Use deep breathing exercises whenever you feel overwhelmed, anxious, or agitated, both at home and in other environments.

9. Seek Professional Help if Needed:

If you find it challenging to regulate your emotions despite practicing these skills, consider seeking support from a mental health professional who can provide personalized guidance and strategies.

By practicing deep breathing exercises regularly, you can develop greater self-awareness, enhance emotional regulation skills, and cultivate a sense of calm and resilience in the face of life's challenges.

Seeking Professional Support

Therapy can be an invaluable resource in addressing the challenges of emotional regulation in anxious attachment recovery. Therapists specializing in attachment issues can offer personalized strategies and support for navigating the complexities of emotional regulation.

The path to recovery from anxious attachment involves confronting and overcoming significant challenges in emotional regulation. By understanding the roots of these difficulties and employing targeted strategies to address them, individuals can make meaningful progress towards more stable and fulfilling relationships. This journey is not only about learning to regulate emotions more effectively but also about building a deeper, more compassionate relationship with oneself. Through patience, perseverance, and support, recovery is not only possible but can open the door to a life of greater emotional resilience and connection.

Strategies for Strengthening Self-Esteem and Identity

Cultivating Self-Compassion

Learning to treat oneself with kindness, understanding, and compassion is a fundamental step in repairing self-esteem. Self-compassion encourages a non-judgmental acceptance of oneself, fostering resilience against the internalized criticism that often accompanies anxious attachment.

Developing Autonomy

Building a sense of autonomy involves engaging in activities and pursuits that reflect one's personal interests and values, independent of a partner's influence.

This can help individuals discover and affirm their identity, reinforcing the notion that their worth is not contingent on their relationship status.

Assertiveness Training

Practicing assertiveness can empower individuals to express their needs, desires, and boundaries within relationships more effectively. This not only enhances self-esteem but also supports the development of healthier, more balanced relationships.

Exploring Personal Values

Reflecting on and defining personal values can serve as a compass for decision-making and identity formation. By identifying what truly matters to them, individuals can align their actions and choices with their core beliefs, fostering a stronger, more cohesive sense of self.

Therapy and Support Groups

Engaging in therapy, particularly with a focus on attachment and self-esteem issues, can provide invaluable guidance and support. Therapists can help individuals unpack the roots of their self-esteem and identity challenges, offering strategies for growth and healing. Support groups offer a sense of community and validation, reminding individuals that they are not alone in their struggles.

Recovering from anxious attachment involves a nuanced understanding of how early relational experiences shape self-esteem and identity. By addressing these foundational aspects of self, individuals can begin to untangle their worth from external validation, embracing a more stable and autonomous sense of self. The journey is one of self-discovery, resilience, and ultimately, transformation, as individuals learn to cultivate a relationship with themselves that is rooted in compassion, authenticity, and self-respect. With commitment and support, recovery opens the door to a life defined not by fear and dependency, but by strength, autonomy, and genuine self-acceptance.

Breaking Free from Co-dependency

Cultivating Self-awareness

The first step towards overcoming co-dependency is recognizing the patterns and behaviors that define it. Reflecting on past and present relationships can reveal how co-dependency manifests in one's life and the impact it has on personal well-being and relationship satisfaction.

Developing Healthy Boundaries

Setting and maintaining healthy boundaries is crucial in dismantling co-dependent patterns. This involves communicating one's needs, limits, and expectations clearly and respectfully, allowing for personal space and autonomy within the relationship.

Fostering Independence

Building a sense of independence and self-sufficiency can help reduce reliance on others for validation and emotional support. Engaging in activities and pursuits that bolster self-esteem and personal fulfillment is key to establishing an individual identity separate from the relationship.

Seeking Professional Support

Therapy can be an invaluable resource in addressing co-dependency and underlying anxious attachment issues. A therapist can provide guidance, support, and strategies to help individuals understand their attachment style, work through co-dependent tendencies, and build healthier relationship patterns.

Prioritizing Self-care

Self-care is an essential component of recovering from co-dependency. It involves taking time for oneself, engaging in activities that promote physical, emotional, and mental well-being, and practicing self-compassion and forgiveness.

Navigating the path from co-dependency to healthier, more balanced relationships is a pivotal aspect of recovering from anxious attachment. By understanding the interplay between anxious attachment and co-dependent behaviors, individuals can begin to address the root causes of their relational dynamics. Through self-awareness, boundary-setting, independence, and professional support, it is possible to break free from the cycles of co-dependency, fostering relationships that are rooted in mutual respect, autonomy, and genuine connection. This journey, though challenging, offers a profound opportunity for growth, healing, and the cultivation of fulfilling, secure attachments.

Embracing Emotional Autonomy

A crucial step in breaking the cycle of co-dependency is achieving emotional autonomy, which involves developing the ability to manage one's emotions independently, without over-reliance on others. Emotional autonomy empowers individuals to seek internal sources of comfort and validation, rather than looking outward to partners or loved ones. This shift is fundamental for those with an anxious attachment style, as it reduces the urgency of their need for constant reassurance and approval.

Reconstructing Self-Identity

Co-dependency often leads to a blurred sense of self, where personal identity becomes deeply entwined with the role one plays in their relationships. Recovering from co-dependency requires a conscious effort to rediscover and reconstruct one's self-identity. This process involves exploring personal interests, values, and goals that are independent of any relationship. By cultivating a strong sense of self, individuals can engage in relationships from a place of wholeness and self-assurance, rather than seeking someone to complete them.

Building Reciprocal Relationships

Part of overcoming co-dependency involves learning to build and maintain reciprocal relationships, where both parties contribute equally to the relationship's health and well-being. This balance ensures that neither partner feels overly burdened or neglected, fostering a dynamic of mutual support and respect. Reciprocal relationships are characterized by open communication, shared decision-making, and an equitable distribution of emotional labor.

Learning to Let Go

An essential, yet often challenging aspect of recovering from co-dependency, is learning to let go of relationships that perpetuate co-dependent dynamics. This may involve ending or redefining relationships that are fundamentally imbalanced or unhealthy. While letting go can be painful, it opens the space for healthier connections and reinforces the individual's commitment to their well-being and recovery.

Engaging in Continuous Personal Growth

Recovery from co-dependency is not a destination but a continuous journey of personal growth. It involves ongoing self-reflection, learning, and adaptation. Individuals are encouraged to seek opportunities for personal development, whether through education, therapy, support groups, or self-help resources. Continuous growth enhances resilience, self-esteem, and the capacity for healthy, autonomous relationships.

The journey out of co-dependency and anxious attachment is both challenging and deeply rewarding. It requires courage, self-compassion, and a commitment to personal growth. By embracing emotional autonomy, reconstructing self-identity, fostering reciprocal relationships, and engaging in continuous personal development, individuals can transcend co-dependent patterns. This transformative process not only enhances personal well-being but also paves the way for more fulfilling and balanced relationships. In the landscape of anxious attachment recovery, overcoming co-dependency stands as a testament to the human capacity for resilience, growth, and the pursuit of genuine, loving connections.

Part V

Building Healthy Relationships

Communicating Needs and Boundaries

Communicating needs and boundaries effectively is crucial for maintaining healthy relationships, fostering mutual respect, and promoting emotional well-being.

Communicating Needs:

Communicating needs involves expressing desires, preferences, and requirements to others in a clear, assertive, and respectful manner.

It involves identifying and articulating what is important to you in various aspects of life, such as relationships, work, and personal development.

Importance:

Helps build trust and understanding in relationships.

Prevents misunderstandings and resentment.

Encourages collaboration and problem-solving.

Supports personal growth and fulfillment.

Strategies:

Self-Reflection: Take time to reflect on your own needs and priorities. Understand what is truly important to you in different areas of your life.

Clear Communication: Express your needs directly and specifically. Use "I" statements to convey your feelings and desires without blaming or accusing others.

Active Listening: Encourage open dialogue by actively listening to others' needs as well. Show empathy and understanding, and validate their experiences.

Negotiation and Compromise: Be open to negotiating and finding compromises that meet the needs of all parties involved. Collaboration fosters stronger relationships and mutual satisfaction.

Follow-Up: Check in periodically to reassess your needs and ensure that they are being met. Be willing to adjust and communicate as circumstances change.

Communicating Boundaries:

Communicating boundaries involves clearly defining and expressing personal limits, expectations, and standards for behavior in relationships and interactions.

It establishes guidelines for how you expect to be treated and what behavior is acceptable or unacceptable to you.

Importance:

Protects personal well-being and emotional safety.

Establishes mutual respect and healthy relationship dynamics.

Prevents exploitation, manipulation, and abuse.

Promotes authenticity and self-respect.

Strategies:

Self-Awareness: Identify your personal boundaries and the reasons behind them. Understand what makes you feel comfortable or uncomfortable in different situations.

Direct Communication: Clearly communicate your boundaries to others in a straightforward and assertive manner. Use assertive language and maintain a calm, confident demeanor.

Consistency: Be consistent in enforcing your boundaries. Set clear consequences for boundary violations and follow through on them when necessary.

Respect Others' Boundaries: Respect the boundaries of others in return. Listen to their needs and preferences, and avoid pressuring or manipulating them into crossing their boundaries.

Seek Support: Seek support from trusted friends, family members, or mental health professionals if you encounter resistance or difficulty in enforcing your boundaries.

Example of Communicating Needs:

Scenario: You're feeling overwhelmed with your workload at work and need additional support from your manager.

Communicating Needs: Schedule a meeting with your manager to discuss your workload and express your need for assistance. Clearly outline the tasks that are causing stress and propose potential solutions, such as delegating tasks or adjusting deadlines.

Example of Communicating Boundaries:

Scenario: A friend frequently makes insensitive jokes about a topic that you find hurtful.

Communicating Boundaries: Have a private conversation with your friend and calmly explain that you find their jokes hurtful and would appreciate it if they could refrain from making them in your presence. Clearly express your boundary and request their cooperation in respecting it.

By effectively communicating needs and boundaries, individuals can foster healthier relationships, maintain their emotional well-being, and create environments of mutual respect and understanding.

Effective communication strategies

Effective communication is essential for building and maintaining healthy relationships, resolving conflicts, and achieving mutual understanding. Here are some strategies for enhancing communication effectiveness:

1. Active Listening:

Focus on the speaker: Give your full attention to the person speaking, making eye contact and showing interest.

Avoid interruptions: Refrain from interrupting or interjecting while the other person is speaking. Let them finish before responding.

Reflective listening: Paraphrase what you've heard to ensure understanding and show that you're engaged in the conversation.

Validate emotions: Acknowledge the speaker's feelings, even if you don't agree with their perspective.

2. Clarity and Conciseness:

Be clear and specific: Express your thoughts and feelings in a straightforward manner, using concise language.

Avoid ambiguity: Clarify any points that may be unclear and ask for clarification if needed.

Stay on topic: Stick to the main point of the conversation and avoid veering off into unrelated subjects.

3. Empathy and Understanding:

Put yourself in their shoes: Try to understand the other person's perspective and empathize with their feelings.

Validate emotions: Acknowledge the validity of the other person's emotions, even if you don't agree with their viewpoint.

Show empathy: Express empathy through your words and actions, demonstrating that you care about the other person's experiences.

4. Nonverbal Communication:

Pay attention to body language: Be aware of your own body language and the body language of the person you're communicating with. Maintain open and relaxed posture.

Use facial expressions: Use facial expressions to convey sincerity, interest, and understanding.

Gauge reactions: Pay attention to the other person's nonverbal cues to gauge their reactions and adjust your communication accordingly.

5. Respect and Validation:

Respect differences: Acknowledge and respect differences in opinions, beliefs, and values.

Avoid judgment: Refrain from making judgments or criticizing the other person's thoughts or feelings.

Validate feelings: Validate the other person's feelings and experiences, even if you don't share the same perspective.

6. Assertiveness:

Express yourself confidently: Communicate your thoughts, feelings, and needs assertively, using "I" statements.

Set boundaries: Clearly communicate your boundaries and assert your right to be treated with respect.

Be respectful: Assertiveness does not mean aggression. Maintain a respectful tone and demeanor in your communication.

7. Practice Active Problem-Solving:

Focus on solutions: Instead of dwelling on problems, focus on finding solutions together.

Collaborate: Involve the other person in problem-solving discussions and work together to find mutually agreeable solutions.

Be open to compromise: Be willing to negotiate and find compromises that meet both parties' needs.

8. Feedback:

Provide constructive feedback: Offer feedback in a constructive and non-critical manner, focusing on specific behaviors or actions.

Be receptive to feedback: Be open to receiving feedback from others and use it as an opportunity for growth and improvement.

Express appreciation: Acknowledge and appreciate positive behavior or contributions from others.

9. Practice Patience and Understanding:

Be patient: Practice patience and understanding, especially in challenging or emotionally charged situations.

Take breaks if needed: If the conversation becomes heated or unproductive, take a break to cool off and regroup before continuing.

10. Continuous Improvement:

Reflect on your communication: Regularly reflect on your communication style and effectiveness, and identify areas for improvement.

Seek feedback: Ask for feedback from trusted friends, colleagues, or mentors to gain insights into your communication strengths and weaknesses.

Practice active communication: Practice active communication skills regularly to enhance your effectiveness over time.

By incorporating these strategies into your communication style, you can foster more meaningful connections, resolve conflicts more effectively, and achieve greater mutual understanding in your interactions with others.

Fostering Trust and Intimacy

Fostering trust and intimacy is essential for building strong, meaningful relationships characterized by openness, vulnerability, and emotional connection.

Practice honesty and transparency in your communication. Share your thoughts, feelings, and experiences openly, even when it's difficult.

Listen attentively to your partner's thoughts, feelings, and concerns without judgment or interruption. Show empathy and validate their experiences.

Be willing to be vulnerable and share your innermost thoughts and feelings with your partner. Vulnerability fosters intimacy and deepens emotional connection.

Be consistent in your actions and words. Follow through on your commitments and promises to build trust and reliability.

Be there for your partner when they need you, providing support and reassurance. Consistent availability strengthens trust and security in the relationship.

Respect your partner's boundaries and personal space. Avoid pressuring or coercing them into doing things they're not comfortable with.

Seek to understand your partner's perspective and experiences. Show empathy and compassion towards their feelings and struggles.

Validate your partner's emotions and experiences, even if you don't share the same perspective. Acknowledge their feelings and let them know that you're there for them.

Respond to your partner's emotional needs with empathy and sensitivity. Offer comfort, encouragement, and understanding during times of distress.

Spend quality time together engaging in activities you both enjoy. Shared experiences create bonding opportunities and strengthen emotional connection.

Create memorable experiences together, such as traveling, trying new activities, or simply spending time in each other's company.

Trust takes time to build and develop. Be patient and understanding as you and your partner navigate the process of building trust and intimacy.

Demonstrate trustworthy behavior consistently over time to reinforce trust and reliability in the relationship.

Practice forgiveness and let go of past hurts and grievances. Holding onto resentment can erode trust and intimacy in the relationship.

When conflicts or misunderstandings arise, work together to address them constructively and find resolutions. Apologize when necessary and make efforts to repair the relationship.

Maintain a relationship based on mutual respect and equality, where both partners' needs, desires, and perspectives are valued and considered.

Respect each other's differences and individuality, recognizing that it contributes to the richness and diversity of the relationship.

Express physical affection regularly through hugs, kisses, cuddling, and other gestures of intimacy. Physical touch fosters closeness and emotional connection.

Nurture sexual intimacy by prioritizing each other's pleasure and desires. Open communication about sexual needs and preferences enhances intimacy and satisfaction.

By incorporating these strategies into your relationship, you can create an environment of trust, emotional connection, and intimacy that strengthens your bond and enhances overall relationship satisfaction.

Trust-building exercises

Trust-building exercises are activities designed to promote mutual trust, understanding, and connection between individuals or groups. These exercises often focus on fostering open communication, empathy, vulnerability, and collaboration. Here are some examples of trust-building exercises:

1. Sharing Personal Stories:

Participants take turns sharing personal stories or experiences with the group. This exercise promotes vulnerability and deepens understanding among group members.

2. Blindfolded Trust Walk:

One participant wears a blindfold while another guides them through an obstacle course or unfamiliar environment. This activity builds trust and encourages communication and reliance on one another.

3. Trust Fall:

One participant stands with their back to the group, crosses their arms over their chest, and falls backward, trusting that the group will catch them. This exercise promotes trust and teamwork.

4. Group Problem-Solving:

Participants work together to solve a complex problem or complete a challenging task. This activity encourages collaboration, communication, and mutual support.

5. Team-Building Games:

Various team-building games, such as the human knot or the minefield game, require participants to work together to achieve a common goal. These games promote trust, cooperation, and problem-solving skills.

6. Trust-Building Circles:

Participants stand in a circle and take turns sharing something they appreciate or admire about the person standing next to them. This activity fosters positive regard and strengthens relationships within the group.

7. Trust-building Workshops:

Structured workshops or seminars focusing on trust-building techniques, such as active listening, conflict resolution, and empathy training. These workshops provide participants with practical skills for building trust in various contexts.

8. Vulnerability Exercises:

Participants engage in activities encouraging vulnerability, such as sharing fears or insecurities with the group. This exercise fosters empathy, understanding, and emotional connection.

9. Feedback Circles:

Participants form small groups and take turns providing constructive feedback to one another. This activity promotes trust and openness by encouraging honest communication and mutual support.

10. Reflective Listening:

Participants pair up and take turns sharing their thoughts and feelings on a given topic while their partner practices reflective listening. This exercise promotes empathy, validation, and active listening skills.

Tips for Effective Trust-Building Exercises:

Ensure the physical and emotional safety of all participants.

Encourage open communication and active participation.

Provide opportunities for reflection and debriefing after each exercise.

Tailor exercises to the specific needs and dynamics of the group.

Foster a supportive and non-judgmental environment throughout the activities.

By incorporating trust-building exercises into group settings, teams, or relationships, individuals can strengthen bonds, improve communication, and cultivate a culture of trust and collaboration.

Part VI

Special Topics

Understanding avoidant attachment

Understanding avoidant attachment involves recognizing its characteristics, origins, and impact on relationships. Here's how to gain a deeper understanding:

1. Recognize Characteristics:

Emotional Detachment: Individuals with avoidant attachment tend to keep their emotions at a distance and may struggle to express vulnerability.

Fear of Intimacy: There's often a deep-seated fear of getting too close to others, leading to discomfort with emotional closeness.

Independence: They prioritize self-sufficiency and may resist relying on others for support or reassurance.

Dismissal of Emotions: Avoidant individuals may downplay or suppress their emotions as a coping mechanism.

2. Explore Origins:

Childhood Experiences: Avoidant attachment often stems from inconsistent or unavailable caregiving in childhood. This lack of reliable emotional support can lead children to develop self-reliant coping strategies.

Attachment Theory: Understanding attachment theory can provide insight into how early experiences shape adult attachment styles. Recognize that avoidant attachment is a learned response to perceived emotional unavailability or rejection.

3. Assess Relationship Patterns:

Intimate Relationships: Look at patterns in romantic relationships, such as difficulty with commitment, fear of emotional closeness, or a tendency to withdraw when intimacy deepens.

Communication Dynamics: Notice communication patterns, such as avoidance of emotional topics, reluctance to express needs, or a preference for maintaining emotional distance.

Impact on Partner: Consider how avoidant attachment may affect your partner or others, leading to feelings of rejection, frustration, or loneliness.

4. Practice Empathy and Compassion:

Put Yourself in Their Shoes: Understand the underlying fears and insecurities driving avoidant behavior. Recognize that it's not a deliberate attempt to hurt you but a defense mechanism.

Validate Their Experience: Acknowledge their feelings and experiences, even if you don't fully understand or agree with them. Validate their need for space and independence without judgment.

5. Encourage Open Communication:

Create a Safe Space: Foster an environment where your partner feels comfortable expressing their thoughts and feelings without fear of judgment or rejection.

Encourage Vulnerability: Encourage your partner to open up and share their emotions, but respect their boundaries and pace.

Use "I" Statements: Express your needs and feelings using "I" statements to avoid triggering defensiveness or withdrawal.

6. Set Realistic Expectations:

Acceptance: Recognize that changing attachment patterns takes time and effort. Be patient and realistic in your expectations for growth and progress.

Instead of trying to change your partner, nurture emotional connection and build trust over time.

7. Seek Professional Help:

Therapy: Consider couples therapy or individual counseling to explore attachment-related issues, improve communication skills, and develop strategies for building healthier relationships.

Self-Reflection: Engage in self-reflection to identify your attachment style and how it interacts with your partner. Recognize patterns in your behavior and emotions.

8. Practice Self-Care:

Boundaries: Set boundaries to protect your emotional well-being and prevent burnout in the relationship.

Self-Compassion: Be kind to yourself and practice self-compassion as you navigate the challenges of understanding and supporting an avoidant partner.

By understanding avoidant attachment and its impact on relationships, you can approach your partner with empathy, patience, and support, fostering a stronger connection and creating a more fulfilling relationship for both of you.

Anxious Attachment in Different Types of Relationships

Anxious attachment can manifest differently in various relationships, including romantic partnerships, friendships, and familial connections. Here's how anxious attachment may present itself in different kinds of relationships:

Romantic Relationships

Fear of Abandonment: Anxious individuals often fear being abandoned or rejected by their romantic partners. They may constantly seek reassurance of their partner's love and commitment.

Overdependence: Anxious individuals may rely heavily on their romantic partner for emotional support and validation, sometimes to the point of becoming clingy or possessive.

Jealousy and Insecurity: Anxious attachment can lead to heightened jealousy and insecurity in romantic relationships. Individuals may interpret minor signs of disinterest or distance as evidence of impending rejection.

Hyperawareness of Relationship Status: Anxious individuals tend to be hyperaware of the status of their relationship and may interpret ambiguous signals from their partner as signs of impending abandonment.

Friendships and family dynamics

Much like in romantic relationships, anxious attachment in friendships is characterized by an intense fear of abandonment, a high need for validation, and sensitivity to the moods and actions of friends. It stems from the attachment theory, which suggests that the bonds we form with our caregivers in early childhood can influence our relationships throughout life. People with an anxious attachment style often worry about their friendships, fearing rejection or believing their friends do not value them. This can lead to behaviors that aim to seek reassurance or clinginess, potentially straining relationships.

Critical Characteristics of Anxious Attachment in Friendships

High Need for Reassurance: Individuals with an anxious attachment style may require constant validation and reassurance from their friends to feel secure in the relationship.

Fear of Abandonment: They often worry about being left out or abandoned and may interpret minor actions or cues as signs of impending rejection.

Sensitivity to Friend's Moods and Actions: People with anxious attachment are highly attuned to their friends' behaviors and moods, often reacting strongly to perceived signs of disinterest or annoyance.

Difficulty with Boundaries: They may struggle to maintain healthy boundaries by becoming too involved in their friends' lives or allowing their friends to overstep their boundaries.

Conflict Aversion: Anxious individuals may avoid conflicts or have difficulty expressing their needs and wants, fearing that disagreements will lead to rejection or the end of the friendship.

Overanalyzing Relationships: They tend to overanalyze texts, conversations, and interactions, often reading negative meanings into neutral situations.

Managing Anxious Attachment in Friendships

Managing anxious attachment involves developing a greater self-awareness and working towards secure attachment behaviors. This can include:

Building Self-Esteem: Focusing on personal growth and self-esteem can help reduce dependency on friends for validation.

Communicating Needs: Learning to communicate needs and feelings effectively can help establish more explicit expectations and boundaries.

Seeking Support: Therapy or counseling can provide strategies for managing anxiety and fostering healthier relationships.

Mindfulness and Self-Compassion: Mindfulness can help manage intense emotions and reactions, while self-compassion encourages a kinder, more forgiving attitude towards oneself.

Expanding Social Circles: Diversifying social connections can reduce the pressure on friendships and provide a more balanced support system.

Understanding and addressing anxious attachment in friendships is crucial for building stronger, healthier relationships. Developing more secure and fulfilling connections requires patience and effort in self-reflection and communication with friends. Let's consider a fictional example that illustrates anxious attachment in a friendship:

The Story of Alex and Jordan

Alex has an anxious attachment style and is best friends with Jordan. Alex values their friendship deeply but often worries about the stability of their connection. Despite Jordan's reassurances and consistent behavior, Alex fears Jordan will find new friends and leave them behind.

Example Behaviors and Situations

Constant Need for Reassurance: Alex often texts Jordan, seeking affirmation of their friendship. After spending time together, Alex might say, "Did you have a good time today? I hope I wasn't too boring." Even after positive affirmations from Jordan, Alex still doubts the security of their friendship.

Overanalyzing Interactions: When Jordan posts pictures on social media with other friends and doesn't immediately respond to Alex's texts, Alex starts to panic, thinking Jordan prefers those other friends. This leads to a spiral of negative thoughts, even though Jordan's behavior is simply the result of a busy schedule.

Fear of Expressing Needs: Alex often feels left out when Jordan makes plans with other friends but is afraid to express their desire for more inclusion. Alex worries that doing so might come off as needy or clingy, potentially pushing Jordan away.

Difficulty with Boundaries: Alex needs help to respect this request when Jordan asks for some space to focus on personal issues. They continue to reach out frequently, fearing that the distance will become permanent. This behavior stems from Alex's fear of abandonment, not from disregarding Jordan's needs.

Sensitivity to Mood Changes: After a day out, if Jordan seems quieter than usual, Alex immediately assumes it's because of something they did or said rather than considering other factors, like Jordan being tired or preoccupied with personal thoughts.

Impact on the Friendship

This anxious attachment behavior puts a strain on the friendship. Jordan feels pressured and overwhelmed by Alex's constant need for reassurance and the inability to respect boundaries. Meanwhile, Alex's fears and insecurities prevent them from enjoying the friendship and contribute to a cycle of anxiety and misunderstanding.

Addressing Anxious Attachment

For their friendship to thrive, Alex needs to work on building self-esteem and trust in the relationship. Engaging in open and honest communication about their fears and needs can help. Additionally, Alex might benefit from individual therapy to explore the roots of their anxious attachment style and develop healthier coping strategies. Meanwhile, Jordan can support Alex by setting clear boundaries and offering reassurance while encouraging Alex's journey towards a more secure attachment style.

Familial Relationships:

Dependency on Family Members: Anxious individuals may rely heavily on their family members for emotional support and validation. They may feel anxious or distressed when separated from their family members for extended periods.

Fear of Disconnection: Anxious attachment can lead individuals to fear disconnection or estrangement from their family members. They may go to great lengths to maintain close ties with their family and feel anxious or insecure when their family members are unavailable or unresponsive.

Conflict Avoidance: Anxious individuals may avoid conflict with their family members for fear of damaging the relationship. They may suppress their needs and desires to maintain harmony within the family.

In familial relationships, anxious attachment can manifest in various dynamics, such as between parent and child, among siblings, or within extended family relationships. Let's explore an example that illustrates anxious attachment within a parent-child relationship.

The Story of Maya and Her Mother, Elena

Maya, a college student, exhibits signs of anxious attachment in her relationship with her mother, Elena. Growing up, Maya felt that her mother's attention and affection depended on her achievements and behavior. As a result, Maya developed a deep-seated fear of disappointing her mother and a constant need for her approval and reassurance.

Example Behaviors and Situations

Constant Need for Reassurance: Maya frequently calls and texts her mother to share details about her daily life, seeking approval for her decisions, big and small. After each call or message, she anxiously awaits her mother's positive feedback to feel secure.

Fear of Making Decisions Alone: Maya struggles with making decisions independently, fearing that choosing "wrong" could lead to her mother's disapproval. Even for minor decisions, like selecting courses for the semester, Maya needs her mother's input to proceed.

Hypersensitivity to Criticism: Any hint of criticism or disappointment from Elena triggers intense anxiety in Maya. For example, if Elena comments that Maya could study more or make different choices, Maya perceives it as a profound failure, leading to distress and efforts to "make things right."

Avoidance of Conflict: Maya goes to great lengths to avoid conflict with her mother. She often suppresses her desires or opinions that might diverge from Elena's views, fearing that disagreement could jeopardize their relationship.

Reassurance-seeking Beyond Normal: Before any significant academic or life event, Maya seeks excessive reassurance from Elena, believing that her mother's encouragement is crucial for her success. This dependency limits Maya's ability to trust in her capabilities.

Impact on the Relationship

This dynamic puts a strain on both Maya and Elena. Elena feels overwhelmed by the constant need for reassurance and guidance, while Maya's reliance on her mother's approval hampers her journey toward independence and self-confidence. The relationship becomes unbalanced, with Maya's fears and anxieties dictating the interactions and preventing her from developing a secure sense of self.

Addressing Anxious Attachment in Familial Relationships

For the relationship to move towards a healthier dynamic, Maya and Elena must recognize and address the patterns contributing to anxious attachment. Maya could benefit from therapy to explore the origins of her anxieties and learn strategies for building self-esteem and independence. Simultaneously, Elena can work on encouraging Maya's autonomy by offering support without over-involvement, helping Maya feel secure even when making independent decisions.

Open communication about their feelings and needs can help Maya and Elena establish a more balanced relationship. By setting healthy boundaries and fostering mutual respect, they can shift towards a dynamic supporting Maya's independence journey while maintaining a solid and supportive familial bond.

Professional relationships

Anxious individuals may seek constant approval and validation from their coworkers or supervisors. They may feel anxious or distressed when they receive negative feedback or criticism.

Anxious attachment can lead individuals to fear failure or disapproval in the workplace. They may become worried or stressed when faced with new challenges or responsibilities.

Anxious individuals may have difficulty setting boundaries with their coworkers or supervisors. They may feel obligated to take on additional tasks or responsibilities to gain approval or avoid conflict.

In all types of relationships, anxious attachment can lead to heightened sensitivity to rejection, fear of abandonment, and difficulty trusting others. However, individuals with anxious attachments can learn to cultivate healthier relationship dynamics and develop more secure attachment patterns with self-awareness, introspection, and support. Therapy, particularly attachment-focused therapy, can be a valuable resource for individuals seeking to address anxious attachment issues and improve their relationships.

The Story of Simon and His Manager, Claire

Simon is a dedicated employee with an anxious attachment style, affecting his relationship with his manager, Claire. Simon is highly competent in his role, but his need for validation and fear of negative evaluation significantly impact his work life.

Example Behaviors and Situations

Constant Need for Reassurance: Simon frequently seeks out Claire for reassurance about his performance. After submitting reports or completing projects, he immediately asks for feedback, needing to hear that his work meets or exceeds expectations to feel secure.

Fear of Negative Evaluation: Simon is overly sensitive to critique or constructive feedback from Claire. He tends to interpret even minor suggestions.

Difficulty with Autonomy: Despite his experience and skill, Simon needs to work on making independent decisions with Claire's approval. He worries that taking the initiative might lead to mistakes that could disappoint her or harm his standing in the company.

Overanalyzing Interactions: Simon tends to overanalyze emails and conversations with Claire, reading into the tone and choice of words for signs of dissatisfaction. This often leads to unnecessary stress and can hinder his focus and productivity.

Avoidance of Conflict: Simon avoids any situation leading to disagreement or conflict with Claire. He goes out of his way to align his opinions and decisions with what he perceives Claire wants, even if it means setting aside his professional judgment.

Impact on the Professional Relationship

This dynamic can be challenging for both Simon and Claire. Simon's constant need for reassurance and approval can be draining for Claire and might limit her ability to manage her team effectively. It also prevents Simon from fully developing his professional autonomy and confidence, potentially stalling his career progression.

Addressing Anxious Attachment in Professional Relationships

For the professional relationship to thrive, Simon and Claire must address the underlying issues.

Professional Development for Simon: Engaging in professional development opportunities can help Simon build confidence in his skills and decision-making abilities. Mentorship programs or workshops focused on self-efficacy and autonomy in the workplace could be particularly beneficial.

Feedback and Communication: Claire can help by providing clear, consistent feedback and encouraging a culture of open communication. Setting specific times for feedback discussions can help Simon adjust his expectations and reduce his anxiety around performance evaluations.

Boundaries and Autonomy: Establishing clear boundaries around communication and decision-making can empower Simon. Claire might encourage him to take the lead on specific projects, providing a safety net without micromanaging, to foster his sense of independence.

Self-awareness and Coping Strategies: Simon could benefit from exploring strategies to manage his anxiety, such as mindfulness or cognitive-behavioral approaches. Recognizing his anxious attachment style and its impact on his professional relationships can be the first step towards healthier workplace dynamics.

By addressing anxious attachment behaviors, Simon and Claire can work towards a more balanced and productive professional relationship, where Simon feels secure in his role, and Claire can effectively manage her team.

Conclusion

Empowerment Through Recovery

"Anxious Attachment Recovery" serves as a beacon of hope and guidance for individuals navigating the challenging journey of recovery from various life struggles, whether it be addiction, trauma, mental health disorders, or other adversities. Throughout this book, readers have been equipped with practical tools, insightful wisdom, and compassionate encouragement to embark on a transformative path toward healing, growth, and empowerment.

As we draw our journey together to a close, it's essential to reflect on the profound lessons learned and the transformative power of resilience and self-discovery. Through the pages of "Empowerment Through Recovery," readers have discovered the following key insights:

The Power of Self-Awareness: By delving into the depths of their inner selves, readers have learned to confront their fears, traumas, and limiting beliefs, fostering a deeper understanding of their strengths and vulnerabilities.

Cultivating Resilience: Through the stories of resilience shared within these pages, readers have gleaned invaluable lessons on overcoming adversity, embracing setbacks as opportunities for growth, and summoning the inner strength to persevere in the face of life's challenges.

Building Healthy Relationships: From exploring the dynamics of attachment styles to learning effective communication strategies, readers have gained the tools to cultivate meaningful connections, set boundaries, and navigate the complexities of interpersonal relationships with empathy and grace.

Embracing Self-Care: By prioritizing self-care practices, readers have discovered the importance of nurturing their physical, emotional, and spiritual well-being, replenishing their energy reserves, and enhancing their capacity for resilience and self-compassion.

Fostering Empowerment: Armed with newfound knowledge and self-awareness, readers have embarked on a journey of empowerment, reclaiming their agency, rewriting their narratives, and stepping into their fullest potential with courage and conviction.

As readers continue their journey beyond the pages of this book, may they carry with them the lessons learned, the wisdom gained, and the unwavering belief in their inherent capacity for healing and transformation. May "Empowerment Through Recovery" serve as a steadfast companion and source of inspiration, guiding readers toward a life of authenticity, purpose, and empowerment. Remember, the path to recovery is not without twists and turns, but with resilience, self-compassion, and a commitment to growth, the possibilities for transformation are endless.

Celebrating progress and growth

In pursuing personal development and self-improvement, it's easy to become fixated on the end goals, overlooking the journey's significance. However, amidst the ups and downs of life, it's crucial to pause, reflect, and celebrate the progress and growth we've achieved along the way. Whether large or small, every step forward is a testament to our resilience, determination, and capacity for transformation.

Acknowledging the Journey

Life is a journey marked by countless milestones, challenges, and opportunities for growth. Each experience shapes us, molding us into the individuals we are meant to become. Yet, in our relentless pursuit of success and achievement, we often overlook our progress and the lessons we've learned.

Celebrating progress is about acknowledging the journey—the highs, the lows, and everything in between. It's about recognizing the courage to step out of our comfort zones, the resilience to overcome obstacles, and the wisdom we gain from our experiences.

Embracing Self-Compassion

At the heart of celebrating progress lies self-compassion—the gentle acknowledgment of our humanity, imperfections, and vulnerabilities. Too often, we are our own harshest critics, dwelling on our shortcomings and failures instead of honoring our efforts and achievements.

Embracing self-compassion means treating ourselves with kindness, understanding, and empathy, especially during times of difficulty or setback. It means reframing our inner dialogue from one of self-criticism to one of self-encouragement and self-love.

Cultivating Gratitude

Gratitude is a powerful tool for celebrating progress and growth. It shifts our focus from what we lack to what we have, fostering a sense of abundance, contentment, and joy. By cultivating gratitude, we learn to appreciate the blessings and opportunities surrounding us, whether small or insignificant.

Take a moment each day to reflect on the progress you've made, the challenges you've overcome, and the blessings you've received. Keep a gratitude journal, jotting down three things you're thankful for daily. Over time, you'll notice a shift in your perspective as gratitude becomes a guiding force.

Setting Milestones and Celebrating Achievements

Setting milestones is a powerful way to track progress and stay motivated on your growth journey. Break down your goals into smaller, more manageable tasks, and celebrate each milestone you reach. Whether completing a project, getting a fitness goal, or mastering a new skill, take the time to acknowledge and celebrate your achievements.

Sharing Successes with Others

Celebrating progress is a personal endeavor and an opportunity to share your successes with others. Whether it's with friends, family, or colleagues, sharing your achievements allows you to bask in the joy of your accomplishments and inspire others to pursue their own goals and aspirations.

In a world that often values achievement over progress, it's essential to take a step back and celebrate the journey—the growth, the setbacks, and the victories. By embracing self-compassion, cultivating gratitude, setting milestones, and sharing successes with others, we can honor the progress we've made and continue to strive for growth, fulfillment, and self-discovery along the path of life. Remember, progress is not always linear, but every step forward, no matter how small, is a cause for celebration. So, let's raise a toast to our journey, embracing growth and celebrating our progress thus far.

Looking forward to secure, fulfilling relationships

In our quest for connection and belonging, few pursuits are as profound or rewarding as the journey toward secure and fulfilling relationships. Whether in our friendships, romantic partnerships, or familial connections, the desire for deep, meaningful bonds is a universal human longing that shapes our sense of self, happiness, and overall well-being. As we embark on this journey, we are filled with hope, anticipation, and a deep-seated desire to cultivate relationships that nurture our souls and enrich our lives.

In pursuing secure and fulfilling relationships, we embark on a journey of hope, growth, and self-discovery. It is a journey filled with challenges, setbacks, and moments of profound connection and joy. As we navigate the twists and turns of this journey, let us embrace each experience with an open heart and a willingness to learn and grow together. Ultimately, the journey itself—the moments of laughter, the tears shed, and the bonds forged—makes the destination worth the wait.

Step forward

Exercises and Practices for Daily Life

Affirmations are powerful tools for transforming negative thought patterns and cultivating a mindset of self-worth, security, and love. In the journey of anxious attachment recovery, affirmations can serve as daily reminders of your inherent value, deservingness of love, and capacity for healthy relationships. In this chapter, we'll explore affirmations specifically tailored to support your journey of healing and growth.

Affirmations for Self-Worth:

"I am worthy of love and belonging, just as I am."

"I deserve to be treated with kindness, respect, and compassion."

"I embrace my imperfections and recognize them as part of my unique beauty."

"I am enough, exactly as I am now."

Affirmations for Security:

"I trust in the strength of my relationships and my ability to navigate challenges."

"I release the need for control and embrace the uncertainty of life with grace and courage."

"I am safe and secure, both within myself and in my connections with others."

"I let go of fear and embrace vulnerability as a pathway to deeper intimacy and connection."

"I am resilient and capable of overcoming any obstacles that come my way."

Affirmations for Healthy Boundaries:

"I honor my needs and boundaries, communicating them assertively with others."

"I deserve to have my boundaries respected and honored by those around me."

"I release the need to please others at the expense of my well-being."

"I trust in my ability to say 'no' when necessary and prioritize self-care."

"I create space for healthy and supportive relationships by maintaining clear boundaries."

Affirmations for Emotional Healing:

"I forgive myself for past mistakes and embrace the opportunity for growth and transformation."

"I release the pain of past wounds and open myself to the healing power of love and compassion."

"I am resilient and capable of overcoming any challenges that come my way."

"I let go of the need for perfection and embrace my journey of self-discovery with patience and kindness."

"I am worthy of love and belonging, and I trust in my ability to create fulfilling relationships."

Incorporating these affirmations into your daily routine can support your journey of anxious attachment recovery, fostering a mindset of self-worth, security, and resilience. Choose the affirmations that resonate most deeply with you, and repeat them regularly with conviction and intention. Remember, the power of affirmations lies in their ability to shift your thoughts and beliefs, empowering you to cultivate healthier relationships with yourself and others.

Made in United States
North Haven, CT
30 April 2024

51940796R00072